*What they're saying about*

# A Funny Thing Happened at the Interview

"George Bernard Shaw said, 'When a thing is funny, search for a hidden truth.' This book is both: funny and oh so true."

**V. John Guthery,** President
Seagate Associates/Outplacement International

"A unique book taking a different and effective approach. The use of real-life stories communicates the basics of job interviewing in a way that is fresh, entertaining and powerful."

**Robert W. Bly,** Author
*Creative Careers: Real Jobs in Glamour Fields* (Wiley)

"Humorous and insightful accounts of interviews…. The end-of-story wrap-up is a unique approach to teaching valuable lessons…. An enjoyable and worthwhile book to read. A must read for any job hunter! "

**Sandra Grabczynski,** Director of Recruiting
The University of Michigan
Office of Career Development

"Where was this book when I was interviewing for my new Program Coordinator?! *A Funny Thing Happened at the Interview* offers important nuggets of real advice along with the chuckles. If you're searching or hiring for a job, buy this book. Believe me, it will help you make it through with your humor and sanity intact. I'm giving one to everyone I know!"

**Gina Kazimir,** Executive Director
Cecil County (Maryland) Arts Council, Inc.

D0619939

"I couldn't put this book down. Interviewing for a job is one of life's great traumatic hurdles that we all share, and the stories presented here tap into that common experience.... reader[s] will be aware that these catastrophes could have happened to them, and eternally grateful that they didn't!"

**Frank Fox,** Executive Director
Professional Association of Résumé Writers

"...a lively, anecdotal stroll through interviews from hell ... a welcome antidote to all those serious tomes that never seem to acknowledge that job applicants are flesh and blood."

**Gary Blake,** Co-author
*Creative Careers* (Wiley)
*Dream Jobs* (Wiley)
Director, The Communication Workshop

"A fabulous book. I enjoyed it and laughed uproariously at some of the incidents.... A worthwhile contribution for all job hunters and employers ... very funny and at the same time very useful."

**Robert Krell,** President
Creative Council

"These funny and interesting anecdotes remind us not only that a sense of humor is important in the sometimes all-too-serious pursuit of a job, but also that out of the ashes of seeming disaster, a true opportunity may bloom."

**Larry Young,** Director
Office of Career Services,
Fairleigh Dickinson University

"*A Funny Thing Happened at the Interview* is a wonderful collection of stories about searching for a job. The stories are diverse, well-written, and instructional. This comprehensive volume of short tales provides a wide range of experiences, usually those to avoid, that can plague job seekers. Most of the stories have a point that we should keep in mind when going for an interview.

"Overall, the book was amusing and upbeat. I liked the variety of stories ... the overall organization of the book ... the many lessons to be learned ... and the appropriate, varied, tone-setting introductory quotes preceding each story. I liked the terse and punchy writing style ... and the graphics representing the main point of the story. And I liked the ending advice which gave each story a positive slant."

**Dale Weinberg,** President
Technically Write

"Proves humor is a great educator. Filled with insights, this book uses frequently hilarious real-life examples to flesh out the rules for using the interview to get hired. The stories are so compelling that I actually read the book from cover to cover, something I'd never done before with a book on interviewing."

**Daniel Lauber,** Author
*Professional's Private Sector Job Finder*
*Government Job Finder*
*Non-Profits' Job Finder*
*The Job Finder's Toolkit*

*"A Funny Thing Happened at the Interview* really is different! Greg Farrell and his team have used a unique strategy to present information that is timely and relevant to job search in the 1990s.... stories and anecdotes are delightful reading, and each of us can relate to the unique circumstances and often hilarious situations we have all faced in our job searches.... should be required reading for all job search professionals."

**Wendy S. Enelow,** Certified Professional Résumé Writer
The Advantage, Inc.,
Executive Résumé and Career Management Center

It's a wonderful book for job seekers faced with so much tension and stress. This light-hearted, funny look at the job-search process empowers, teaches and entertains. I loved it AND it is sorely needed ... a wonderful contribution to the job-search literature.

**Paul Cherry,** President
CareerScore

*"A Funny Thing Happened at the Interview* helps employers to avoid taking themselves so seriously.... Every recruiter will have a Letterman-type top ten from this book. It was fun to read."

**David B. Palmer,** Human Resources Manager
East New York Savings Bank

Mr. Farrell has contributed the one thing that nobody on the job hunt trail can afford to ignore: Humor, the ability to take yourself lightly while taking your pursuit of employment seriously.

In fifteen years of my work with corporations worldwide, I have seen the stories in this book come to life; too often, they have devastating outcomes because the people who experience these trials and traumas of Résumé Wrestling have lost their perspective. *A Funny Thing Happened at the Interview* helps restore that invaluable insight. It also made me laugh. Anyone who can make me laugh while teaching me vital information deserves my recommendation. In fact, they deserve better.

**C.W. Metcalf**
Educator, Author, Lecturer and Fly-fisherman
*Lighten Up...survival skills for people under pressure*
by Metcalf and Felible
(Addison Wesley)

Introducing **Rocky the Résumé**™

# A Funny Thing Happened at the Interview

## Wit, Wisdom and War Stories from the Job Hunt

by **Gregory F. Farrell**

*Foreword by*
**Steve Allen**

**Contributing Authors**
Linda Sue Nathanson
James F. Barrett
Allan Varian
A.L. Sirois

*Illustrations*
Chris McDonough

Edin Books, Inc.
Gillette, New Jersey

*A Funny Thing Happened at the Interview*
*Wit, Wisdom and War Stories from the Job Hunt*

Edin Books, Inc.
P. O. Box 59
Gillette, New Jersey 07933

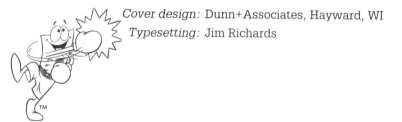

*Cover design:* Dunn+Associates, Hayward, WI
*Typesetting:* Jim Richards

Rocky the Résumé is a trademark of Edin Books, Inc.

Library of Congress Catalog Card Number: 95-060459
Printed in the United States of America

**Publisher's Cataloging in Publication**
*(Prepared by Quality Books Inc.)*

Farrell, Gregory F.
    A funny thing happened at the interview: wit, wisdom and war stories from the job hunt / by Gregory F. Farrell ; foreword by Steve Allen ; contributing authors, Linda Sue Nathanson ... [et al.] ; illustrations, Chris McDonough.
    p. cm.
    Includes index.
    ISBN: 1-887010-00-9

    1. Job hunting.    I. Allen, Steve, 1921-    II. Title.

HF5382.7.F37 1996                    650.14
                                     QB195-20321

*In Memory of Elsie White Farrell,*
*Actress, Writer, Mother*

# Contents

vi

## 5 Unexpected People

## 6 Don't Let the Door Hit You

## 7 There's More to Life

# Steve Allen

Comedian and talk show host, actor, author, composer, pianist, scholar on the art and history of comedy and man-on-the-street interviewer, Steve Allen is one of the most enduring, admired and imitated personalities in the history of television comedy.

Mr. Allen created *The Tonight Show* in 1953 and served as its first host until 1957. He hosted and starred in *The Steve Allen Show* from 1956 to 1964 and hosted *I've Got a Secret* from 1964 to 1967. He was elected to the TV Academy Hall of Fame in 1986.

Mr. Allen has written 44 books including *Make 'Em Laugh, Hi-Ho Steverino!, My Adventures in the Wonderful Wacky World of TV, How to Be Funny, Funny People, More Funny People, The Funny Men* and *The Man Who Turned Back the Clock and Other Short Stories.* He has composed over 5,200 songs.

Thank you for being part of our book.

Linda Sue Nathanson, Ph.D.
*Publisher*

# Foreword
## by Steve Allen

*Given a little time for the pain to subside,
dreadful experiences often can be the basis of funny … stories.*

How to Be Funny
Steve Allen and Jane Wollman, 1992

Humor takes many forms and can be expressed in a thousand different ways. There are no rules about what is funny. Like beauty and pornography, however, you know it when you see it. And I see it in *A Funny Thing Happened at the Interview*.

The funniest stories and best comedy often come from serious and even tragic life experiences. Charlie Chaplin, W. C. Fields, Abbott and Costello, Laurel and Hardy, The Three Stooges, Red Skelton, Sid Caesar, Jackie Gleason, Jerry Lewis, Woody Allen, Neil Simon show us misfortune with all its pain and sorrow … and we laugh.

While it's happening, particularly if it's happening to you, a tragic or embarrassing moment is not funny; but, in the telling, it gets funny, and in the retelling, it gets funnier. That's the heart of *A Funny Thing Happened at the Interview*. This entertaining collection of over 100 fact-based short stories is a gold mine of comedy from the classic American job hunt. These are the war stories that people spend their lives telling and retelling.

Besides their sheer entertainment value, these stories help job hunters and interviewers be alert to the events that can go wrong and right in a job search. It's an awareness-raising book. The stories are about mistakes, blunders, disasters, inspiration, intelligence and luck related to finding or leaving a job.

Perhaps the book's greatest lesson is that when an interview disaster strikes you, it's not a death sentence but your next great story. And you may get the job anyway. Coolth,* composure, and common sense go a long way in turning a bad situation around.

* Mr. Allen's own coinage, as in his *Dumbth: And 81 Ways to Make Americans Smarter,* 1989.

*A Funny Thing Happened at the Interview* is long on experience, short on theory. The settings are wide ranging—from auditorium stage to sound stage, courtroom to barroom, waiting room to computer room, running track to race track, back office to backwoods, one-person office to industrial complex.

Expect laughs, tears, shock, surprise, delight. Savor the cartoons. You'll identify with the characters. You'll be more streetwise. And you may never accept another cup of coffee outside your own home.

*Steve Allen*
*Van Nuys, California*
*1995*

# Preface &
# Acknowledgments

*All for one, one for all, that is our motto.*
Alexandre Dumas, *The Three Musketeers*, 1844

Th**his book is about real-life job transition experiences. Its goal has been to capture the interactions of job hunters with other people, events and circumstances related to finding or leaving a job. While it focuses on the traditional job search interview (before, during and after), it includes stories about exit interviews, sales call interviews and résumé data-gathering interviews.

The stories have different points of view reflecting the voices of those who shared their stories with us—job hunters, hiring managers, résumé writers, human resource professionals, recruiters, consultants and successful former job hunters. The incidents were gathered from over 200 in-person and telephone interviews conducted by Dr. Linda Sue Nathanson and myself. Many of the names and locations have been changed, and in one story, the character is a composite.

This is not a textbook or "how to" book. It's a collection of bite-size chunks for the plane or train, bedroom or bathroom. It was written to entertain and to inform with empowering nuggets of wisdom strewn liberally throughout. To find stories related to particular topics, or to locate a favorite, see the index. For a more conventional "how to" audio tape presentation of interview preparation and strategies, see the ad at the end of this book for *Sock It To Them at the Interview* by James F. Barrett.

Thanks to the following editors, reviewers, researchers and subject matter experts for their valuable comments and contributions: Craig Abramson, Kevin Brady, Sarah J. Fryberger, Ron Hobart (Dunn+Associates, Hayward, WI), Jonathan Kirsch, David Messineo, Barbara Poluhovich, Paula Sirois, Dale Weinberg, David Weinstein, Warren Yarnell.

Many thanks to Frank Fox, Executive Director of the Professional Association of Résumé Writers, and David Opton, publisher of *Exec-U-Net,* who asked their members and readers to send us unusual job search stories.

**xi**

I would like to thank the following people who took the time to share their most interesting stories or bits of wisdom:

Brooke Andrews, A New Beginning, Inc., Mesa, AZ
Carol Armitage
Joi Barlow, CareerSmart, Inc., Norcross, GA
Renae Biale
Gary Burlew
Chris Case
Osa Chapman
Ray Chimileski
Peggy N. Cramer, Assist Business Services, Omaha, NE
Georgia Denny
Russ DiFrancisca
Gene DiGianni
Gil diPierro, COMCITY Business Networks, Somerville, NJ
Kevin Doherty
Michael Donahue
Brian Egan
Rita Eisenberg
Dr. Stuart Eisenberg
John Ercolino
Susan Farrell
Dennis Flood
Robin Folsom, Accent on Résumés, Rockford, IL
Russell Frank, Esq., Warren, NJ
Steven P. Green, CareerPath, Northboro, MA
Mitch Gross
Mary Guindon
Evelyn Horowitz
Hannah Kain
Leona Kardux
Joseph M. Land Sr, Veterans Career Services, Jacksonville, FL
Pamela Lenehan
Debbie Liebeskind
Bob Loria

Harvey Mandel
Don Marantz
Ina Marantz
The Honorable Carmine Marasco
William Marasco
Susan Marasco-Farrell
Shannon McKenzie
Peter Melnick
Frank Montenes
Gary Muenzen
Melanie A. Noonan, Peripheral Pro, West Paterson, NJ
Bill Nordahl
Dennis O'Connor
David Palmer
Karen Palmer
Larry Petcovic
Bernard Powell
Miguel A. Prieto
Jim Richards
Joseph Roberts
Steve Rosenberg
Paul L. Rothstein, PRISM, Watchung, NJ
Judy Ryan
Tony Schiavino, ISES, Inc., Basking Ridge, NJ
Dr. Paul Scollo
Mary Ann Scollo
Howard F. Steinhardt
Darren Tewes
Rev. Stevan J. Thayer, The Center of Being, Inc., Holmdel, NJ
Lynn Vincent, Veterans Career Services, San Diego, CA
Dave Wandelt
Francis White
Barry Wohl, Carolina Career Resources, Charlotte, NC
And several others who pleaded for anonymity.

I'm grateful for the help and support of the talented team that helped bring this book to life: Linda Sue Nathanson, James Barrett, Allan Varian, A.L. Sirois and Chris McDonough. Linda has been the catalyst that launched *A Funny Thing Happened at the Interview*. I thank her for investing her time, interest and energy in the work of a first-time author. We met when I was out of work and went to her for help in revising my résumé. We enjoyed swapping job-hunting stories and soon discovered that we both had articles we had written for *The Wall Street Journal*'s *National Business Employment Weekly* framed on our office walls. We began to collaborate. This book grew out of those meetings.

How two "Leos" were able to work together without killing each other is an amazing story in itself. In a world increasingly dominated by people who will never deviate from the "safe" choice, Linda has proven herself to be a breed apart.

This acknowledgment would not be complete without thanking Steve Allen for generously consenting to write the foreword to this book. It is truly a thrill having a man who has literally "done it all" associated with this work.

Finally, I would like to thank my beautiful wife of fourteen years, Susan Marasco-Farrell. Despite the fact that she insists on hyphenating her name, I still love her dearly. Susan not only contributed several of her own stories, but also put up with the roller-coaster of emotions stemming from my simultaneously writing a book and looking for a job. Susan and our children, Robin and Adam, help me to keep the world in perspective and remember which things in life are truly important and which things just make good stories.

*Gregory F. Farrell*

*Basking Ridge, New Jersey*

*1995*

# Breakfast

*Let them eat cake.*

Marie Antoinette, 1740

**B**ill was a night owl, one of those people who thrive on three or four hours' sleep. At 3 am on any night in college he was usually writing a paper on monetary vs. fiscal policy, or occasionally, guzzling beer with a few other "hypers" watching *I Love Lucy* reruns on the tube. He got an accelerated MBA in eighteen months of day school, night school and summer session.

Now it was time to get a job, his first. He had an interview scheduled for 7 am with an executive vice president of a large investment bank. Bill wasn't keen about the early hour, but he decided to consider it a good sign. These people must be real go-getters, he thought, the time-is-money-and-none-to-waste type, my kind of people.

He arrived downtown with ten minutes to spare. On the corner, he noticed constant activity around the big pushcart under a bright red and yellow umbrella. Everybody was buying "coffee and" as earlybirds arrived and the back-office night shift left for home.

Great idea! he thought. A breakfast meeting and I'll supply the breakfast. Shows I'm thoughtful. It'll keep things equal and informal, eating together. And besides, I'm hungry. So he bought two extra-large containers of coffee, a couple of bagels slathered with cream cheese, and entered the bank at 6:55.

The receptionist (I guess they all start early here!) ushered him and his brown bag into an elegant conference room with two deep leather sofas flanking an oriental rug and a low glass-topped coffee table between them. The executive vice president came in immediately.

"Bill, good to see you. Welcome to our fine old institution. Sit down, sit down, please, and call me Sean." He was younger and friendlier than Bill expected, handsome, athletic and wearing what looked like the most expensive suit he'd ever seen, certainly custom-made and probably from Saville Row in London.

Bill offered breakfast, and Sean was delighted. They sat opposite each other on the couches, opened their coffee and bagels on the table, and began to talk as they ate.

This is the way it's supposed to be, Bill thought. Sean was listening attentively to everything he said, often nodding in agreement. The interview was going so well, in fact, that Bill began to relax. He leaned back into the plush sofa and crossed his legs.

**2**

And his right foot kicked the table, hard. Two extra large coffees cascaded over the oriental rug, Sean's sofa and his suit. *Soaking* Sean's suit would be more accurate. And to top it off, half a bagel landed cream cheese down in Sean's lap.

Bill, of course, was totally flustered. Sean was gracious, but obviously annoyed. He excused himself, and a woman from Personnel finished the interview.

Bill never did hear much of what she said in the next six minutes. He stood and stammered as four maintenance people blotted up the mess and glared at him.

Two days later, Bill received a polite rejection letter from the bank. He was relieved. It could have been a cleaning bill for Sean's suit.

*The consensus among hiring managers is that bringing coffee to an interview is perceived as trying too hard, too personal or unprofessional.*

# Baked Potato

*It was the kind of flop that even made the audience look bad.*

Fred Astaire

**B**ob had all the technical skills, but the job required a lot of presentation work, too. "Very honestly, I'm just not sure how well you'd do on your feet in front of our Board of Directors delivering a strategic plan," said Andrew, not unkindly, as he picked up his glass, savoring the fine wine the Economists Club always served at their luncheon meetings. Andrew turned his attention to the day's speaker being introduced. Bob began to think.

Andrew needs a corporate planner. I want the job. My presentation skills are the question. I have to convince Andrew that I can speak effectively to a group. How?

*"Thank you, ladies and gentlemen. Today, I want to discuss with you...."*

Of course! Here's a built-in audience. I can speak to this group and let Andrew see and hear for himself how effective I can be. I'll be the best damned speaker this club ever had, and get a new job in the process.

After the meeting, Bob sought out the program chairman and volunteered to make the presentation next month, much to the chairman's delight. Speakers were always hard to find. Most members came mainly for the cocktail hour, excellent meal and superb wines. Bob made sure that Andrew would be there.

He prepared diligently — researched the facts, wrote and rewrote his presentation, made slides, practiced in front of the mirror, made his wife listen to it three times.

On the day of his talk, he wore his darkest suit and most conservative tie. He was nervous but ready.

At the cocktail hour, he drank only club soda with lime. Luncheon, as usual, was excellent — roast beef, baked potato and sour cream, fresh string beans and a vintage red wine, which he never touched. Instead, to settle his nerves, he helped himself to a second baked potato and an extra helping of sour cream.

After dessert, the program chairman gave the introduction. Bob rose and stood behind his chair to speak. And it became dreadfully obvious that the double helping of sour cream had been a mistake.

The first dollop of cream probably went into his potato; the second had positively landed in the center of his tie. It was currently working its way slowly down to the tip and onto his pants.

Economists are normally a pretty serious group, but the sight of Bob with sour cream oozing down his tie brought more than a few chuckles. That rattled him, and he launched immediately into his speech.

*"Thank you. My topic today is World Dairy Products and How Prices Are Running."*

An amused voice called out from the back, "Dairy products mostly seem to be running down your tie, Bob!"

Someone offered a napkin and he cleaned up his tie, but now he was completely unnerved, confidence and concentration shattered. He stuttered through his speech. It was so bad it was even painful for the audience. Everyone was relieved when the general discussion began and Bob could sit down.

Bob never got the job offer from Andrew. He had to admit that he really didn't have any presentation skills or he would have turned the situation around by making a joke of it. He also realized that a luncheon club was probably the least painful place to learn that lesson.

From then on, Bob volunteered to give speeches and presentations at every club he belonged to. He got better and better, and today is an accomplished public speaker. He even opens his talks occasionally with the "sour cream tie" story.

*Anyone can fall on his face; it's the getting up again that counts.*

# Luck of the Irish

*No good deed will go unpunished.*

Anonymous

*It was Christmas in New York — lights strung and decorations hung, store windows fully dressed, carols and the smell of roasting chestnuts in the air. Tourists and natives alike smiled as they strolled the avenues. The Spirit of the Season was everywhere.*

I'd been looking for work since July, and now, at Christmas, I was really down — down on my luck and down in the mouth. There's something particularly depressing about Christmas when you don't have a job.

Then I got an interview. It was at 666 Fifth Avenue, right in the center of New York's "Miracle Mile" for shoppers and sightseers — Saks Fifth Avenue, Bergdorf-Goodman, Rockefeller Center, St. Patrick's Cathedral, Radio City Music Hall, all within blocks.

As I walked up Fifth Avenue, coming over from Grand Central Station, I was torn between the Christmas cheer around me and the personal depression inside. Not a good frame of mind for a job interview and I knew it, but how to shake it?

Well, being third-generation Irish and proud of it, an old Irish superstition popped into my head: generosity brings luck. What's to lose, I thought. I could sure use some. So I fished out a five-dollar bill and dropped it with a flourish into a red Salvation Army kettle tended by a bell-ringing Santa.

I felt better already, my luck was sure to change. And it did.

As I stepped off smartly up the avenue, my first step was on the back of a sneaker covering a size-14 foot. It came completely off, the sneaker that is, and was immediately lost amid the high heels and wingtips filling the sidewalk.

The exceptionally large man who owned the sneaker — wearing jeans, black leather jacket, wild black beard and an earring below a woolen ski cap proclaiming "Giants" — looked like he warmed up each day lifting small cars and then worked up to buses and trucks, a walking endorsement of what anabolic steroids can do for you. He was not amused.

**6**

As I started to apologize, hoping he'd say something like "Hey man, accidents happen, forget it," he lunged at my throat. I'd love to tell you I did my Bruce Lee imitation, flattening him with one kick, but my feet actually ran as fast as they could with the one-sneakered gorilla right behind.

It's amazing what a massive adrenaline surge does for you. We weaved up the avenue, in and out of strollers and Santa's helpers, until I hit the lobby of 666 in full stride and squeezed through the closing doors of an elevator.

I deliberately got off at the wrong floor to catch my breath, and then went on to the interview. It was not my best performance. I later heard that I was "too nervous" to handle a high pressure job.

The only good-luck part of that day was that the building had multiple exits, and I was able to leave by a different door. So much for my five-dollar bill and the luck of the Irish.

I never saw my "friend" again, but on the remote chance that he reads this: I'm really sorry I stepped on your foot, and you won't find my address printed anywhere in this book.

*Allow enough time before an interview to regain*
*your composure after an unexpected problem.*

# Eye Contact

*When I make a mistake, it's a beaut.*

Fiorello LaGuardia (1882-1946)

Nursing school was a second chance for Christina. Married, abused and divorced, she now found herself starting over again as a single mother. Working as a nurse would provide her with a good living, and more importantly, a new sense of self-worth.

But she had to get past this interview. She was petrified.

The dean of nursing didn't help. She was late middle-aged, stiff, starched, formal and forbidding. She didn't even smile as her secretary brought Christina in.

Christina knew eye contact was important, so looking the dean straight in the eye, she walked briskly across the office, extended her hand for a firm handshake...and tripped over the wastebasket, flat on her face.

Mortified, she scrambled around on the floor, stuffing crumpled papers back in the basket and stammering apologies.

"Forget those," the dean barked. "Just take a seat, anywhere, and let's begin."

Christina got up and sat in the first seat she saw. The dean stood over her, scowling down, and said, "That's my chair. Please sit over there." Indeed, she saw, the buttons on the telephone and calculator were facing in her direction. She scuttled around the desk.

The dean asked all the normal questions about grades and motivation. One after another they came in rapid fire, no discussion, no notes. Christina answered them all smoothly, but felt sure the dean was rushing her. Just before noon, the interview ended and the dean hadn't smiled or said a kind word once. Christina was devastated.

A few weeks later, though, she was accepted. At school, Christina learned that the dean had a drinking problem and always rushed through her late-morning appointments to get out for a few drinks at lunchtime.

After graduation, Christina spent 12 years as a nurse and was promoted to surgical technician in 1995, working in the operating room.

*Not all bad luck is fatal.*

# Big Old Bomb

*The Edsel is here to stay.*

Henry Ford II

**M**organ Anderson, a teacher, arrived for his 8:30 am interview at an exclusive private school in Greenwich, a wealthy community in southern Connecticut. The campus stood high on a hill with beautiful sloping lawns sparkling in the morning sun. He steered his 13-year-old Lincoln Continental into the drive between the old stone gate posts.

At one time Morgan's Lincoln had been a lovely powder blue, but by the time he bought it, its predominant color was rust. The muffler was perforated, and the whole car rumbled and roared, rattled and squeaked. Friends told him it was like riding in a parade float, complete with its own band.

The headmaster had warned him that parking at the school might be a problem because virtually every student with a driver's license also had a car. It's the symbol of freedom to a wealthy suburban teenager, he said. Still, Morgan gasped as he pulled into the parking lot. It was indeed full. Full of Mercedes sedans and convertibles, BMWs, Fiats, at least one Rolls Royce and something he thought had to be a Lamborghini.

The students were milling around before class doing what teenagers do best: calling to friends, girl- and boy-watching and desperately trying to be "cool." Morgan's car focused their attention. It was twice the size of any other car in the lot and belching black smoke. It created a sensation.

Already nervous about his interview, Morgan didn't like being the center of attention for a hundred or more students he might one day have to teach. On top of that, he couldn't find a parking space. He circled the lot four times, drawing more laughs, jokes, whistles and pointing fingers with each circuit.

Finally, he spotted an empty space next to a Fiat convertible. It looked like a tight squeeze, but he thought he could make it. He never saw the "Compact Cars Only" sign as he hauled the big old Lincoln around.

By this time the students were really enjoying themselves. Morgan did his best to ignore them, but one skinny, pimply-faced boy frantically waving his arms and shouting something about compact cars distracted him and....

Crunch! The awful sound of crumpling, tearing metal! The effect of a

full-sized Lincoln tangling with a Fiat is much like a sledge hammer greeting a raw egg. Morgan could hose off the Continental's bumper and be all right, but there was a deep, jagged furrow plowed down the entire side of the Fiat.

He rolled down the window, and now he could hear the boy. "These spaces are for small cars only, man! What the hell is *wrong* with you?"

All the students, and apparently most of the teachers, came over to survey the scene. The car belonged to the yelling boy, who was now almost crying as he inspected the damage. The other students considered him a "nerd," and that only made the incident more hilarious to them.

It took a good twenty minutes for the teachers to break up the crowd and get the students into class. Morgan had to exchange identification and insurance information with the boy, who told him ominously, "My father's an attorney, you know." That didn't make him feel any better.

When Morgan finally made it to the headmaster's office, the interview didn't go well. No mention was made of the accident, but the man undoubtedly knew every detail. He was cold and formal. He stressed that teachers at the school must not only have impeccable academic credentials, but also be "the Greenwich type."

"I understand, sir," Morgan said quietly. I surely do, he was thinking, and anyone who drives a rusty old bomb and smashes into students' cars isn't the type you're looking for.

As expected, he didn't get the job. He did get two letters postmarked from Greenwich. One was the school's rejection letter. The other was a terse note from the nerd's father, including a large, itemized bill for damages to the Fiat.

*If your ship doesn't fit, you're probably in the wrong harbor.*

# Tex

*Remember the Alamo!*

Colonel Sidney Sherman
at the Battle of San Jacinto, April 1836

Tex was a stereotype of the successful Texas businessman. Except that he lived in Greenwich, Connecticut. His 15 metalworking plants dotted New England, and Bernie wanted to manage one of them.

"C'mon over to mah place for a cookout Friday," Tex told him, "an' we'll talk about it."

Bernie arrived to find a full-scale Texas barbecue in the backyard, and Tex himself cooking up masses of pork chops on a huge open grill.

"Howdy, Bernie," he called across the lawn. "Grab yourse'f a drink. An' sit by me at dinner. We'll talk about that spot in New Hampshire."

Sitting next to Tex, Bernie tried to present his credentials through a rising volume of chatter, mostly about business and baseball. Boisterous laughter and friendly arguments enveloped the tables. Tex kept an ear on them all and regularly interjected his own comments, usually provoking more laughter. Bernie gave up — *later,* he told himself — and eyed the last pork chop on the platter. Everybody was too polite to take it.

Then the lights went out — sudden darkness — and three seconds later, a blood-curdling scream. The lights flickered back on to reveal Bernie's fork sunk into the back of Tex's hand surrounding that last chop.

"Hey, boy, when ah said ah like mah factory managers lean and hungry, ah didn't mean for you to take it so literally!" he groaned with a weak chuckle, shaking his hand gingerly.

Tex did hire Bernie, who still manages the New Hampshire plant very successfully. But at every annual barbecue, he tells about the time Bernie mistook his hand for a pork chop — and every year the fork gets sharper, the wound deeper and the scream louder.

*A social setting, more often than not, is a poor place
to have a first interview. You want to minimize
distractions and have the interviewer focus on you
and your talents. If you have the option,
an office interview is your first choice.*

# Friendly Gesture

*Friendship is far more tragic than love. It lasts longer.*
Oscar Wilde

Cancer is an ugly word. So is melanoma. But that's what I heard when I called Stewart a while back.

I hadn't spoken to him in several months, and I knew he'd been looking for work. And yes, I also wanted to ask if he had any funny interview stories to pass along.

Amazingly, he was in high spirits.

"They took a big slab out of my back a couple of months ago," he told me, "but they say they got it all. That's the good part. It took a helluva bite out of our savings, but it sure changes the way I look at things."

We talked for a while and I decided not even to ask if he had any stories for my book. But he volunteered, no prompting.

"You'll appreciate this one," he said, and went on from there.

As soon as Stewart was up and around after the operation, he got back into his job search full force. He decided not to mention the cancer to any prospective employers for fear it would scare them off. It'll come up in a pre-employment physical, he reasoned, but by then they'll want me.

Stewart got a call about a sales job while his back was still healing. At the interview, he sat very tenderly in a straight-backed wooden chair as the sales manager described the job. As long as he sat up straight and leaned a little forward, away from the chair, his back throbbed but he was fine. He certainly had better posture than ever before.

Anyway, the sales manager was young, much younger than Stewart, and expected all his people to be excited, enthusiastic. "I want you to feel like *shouting* about this job," he fairly shouted himself, "about how much you *love* it."

Stewart thought that kind of pep talk had gone out twenty years ago, but apparently not. He tried to look enthusiastic — leaning forward like this makes me look eager, he thought — but his back was really hurting by then.

"Well, Stewart," the young sales manager ended at last, "that's pretty much my whole rap. Whadda ya think?"

Now Stewart tried to *be* enthusiastic. "Sounds great! Wonderful! Exciting for sure!"

As they were walking out to the lobby, the manager told him, "Stewart, I'm really impressed with your background. You'll be hearing from me

soon." And in the middle of the office, he landed an encouraging but resounding slap on Stewart's back.

*"Aaaaaaaah!"*

"I couldn't hold it in," Stewart told me on the phone. "I never felt such pain in my life! The entire office, thirty people, stopped and stared at me.

"And you know what I did then?"

I tried to guess and couldn't. "No, what?"

"I did it again! He wanted enthusiasm, I gave him enthusiasm. '*AAAAAAH! I LOVE THIS JOB! I WANT IT! AAAH, YES!'*

"That's what a lifetime of sales training does for you," he laughed with me. "It seemed like a good idea at the time, but the people in the office, including the sales manager, just stared at me. Like I escaped from a funny farm.

"He walked me to the lobby in absolute silence. Not another word. He even stayed away from me all the way out, like I might turn violent or something."

I laughed again. "Did you ever hear from them?"

"Nope, not a word. I think they all ran out and gargled when I left."

Stewart is fully recovered now, and he had several interviews scheduled when I spoke with him.

*Luck, good or bad, can play a pivotal role in an interview.*
*If this one doesn't work out, keep looking.*

# More Than a Game

*Who can think and hit at the same time?*

Lawrence (Yogi) Berra

Ryan was an accountant, and after two weeks on the job at the big car company, he desperately wanted to become "part of the team." When the intracompany softball league sign-up sheet was posted, he put his name right at the top. He was a good athlete, and this was his chance.

Arriving at the first game, he was a little surprised to find the beer keg and barbecue pit getting much more attention than the batting cage. The teams were co-ed too.

"Are you a player or a drinker, Ryan?" asked the captain, who was also the chief engineer, a lot more friendly here than on the job.

"A player," Ryan answered, eager to show his skill.

"Good. We need a catcher. I'll put you in the line-up right away."

The game finally started, after much beer and sausages. The socializing continued on the field as well as off.

At Ryan's first turn at bat, he hit a sure single that he wanted to stretch into a double. The centerfielder scooped up the ball and lobbed it in toward the second baseman (or basewoman), a petite blonde named Suzie, the young wife of a senior-level vice president. Wearing a baseball cap and oversized fielder's mitt, she was jumping up and down waving her arms for the ball...and, against all the rules of softball, blocking the basepath.

Ryan bore down on her at full speed as the ball approached.

Make the play! he resolved. Show 'em you're an athlete.

He slid safely into second, slamming Suzie's legs out from under and sending her sprawling in the dirt. Total silence covered the field. Several players helped her limp off to the bench. Everyone stared at Ryan.

When the game resumed, the next batter singled, but nobody congratulated Ryan as he crossed the plate. The captain took him out.

Two weeks later Ryan was laid off in a general cutback.

*The best way to join the team—be it softball or software—
is to learn the corporate culture and get to know the people.
Avoid throwing your weight around until you do.*

# With a Jolt

*There is no such thing as chance; what to us seems merest
accident springs from the deepest source of destiny.*

Friedrich von Schiller (1759-1805)

*Car interiors of the commuter trains into New York City
haven't changed much. They have two-person bench seats
with reversible upright back rests down both sides of a
center aisle. At the end of the line, conductors reverse the
back rests so passengers heading in the other direction can
ride facing forward. A one-inch clearance separates the
seat back from the bench.*

L ike other mornings as I waited for the 7:18, the platform was
crowded. Newspapers shielded faces from the world and attaché cases stood close at heel. As the train arrived, the usual
few latecomers dashed up and jostled to buy coffee that would last them
into Hoboken, New Jersey where we'd all board the PATH subway for
lower Manhattan.

I took my usual window seat midway back in the third car and a
young man sat down beside me. He set a brand new leather briefcase
open on the floor between us. It was a true briefcase, with the opening at
the top and buckle-and-strap closures, the kind that lawyers and profes-
sors usually carry. Not a regular commuter, I saw, as he gave the conduc-
tor a single ticket and I passed over my cut-rate commuter book.

Oh, to have that kind of energy so early in the morning, I thought, as
he dug in and out of that bag furiously, reading and rereading everything,
and mumbling to himself as if rehearsing.

Now, I'm not overly curious by nature, but privacy is in short supply
on a commuter train. I couldn't help noticing that his briefcase was stuffed
with résumés, letters of recommendation, college transcripts and the Help
Wanted pages. Probably psyching himself up for a job interview, I concluded, and good luck to you, son. I went back to my newspaper.

At the next stop, an older woman with a styrofoam cup three-quar-
ters full of steaming coffee sat down in front of the young man and
propped the cup on the seat as she searched her purse for her ticket.

The train started with a jolt and the cup tipped over, spilling coffee
through the space between the seat and back rest and into the young

man's open briefcase. It was truly amazing. Not a drop hit the floor. The entire contents poured directly into the briefcase.

"Oh no!" he screamed, followed by some very colorful and crudely descriptive language as he scrambled to empty the bag. The lady was obviously embarrassed and distressed, apologizing profusely. But the damage was done. The contents of the briefcase were thoroughly soaked.

The young man spent the rest of the trip blotting his wet résumés and letters with his handkerchief, mine and a few others kindly offered. The coffee stains, however, were on those papers forever. There was nothing anyone could say. Sympathy wouldn't help.

When the train reached Hoboken, I got off and took the PATH subway to the World Trade Center as usual. I never saw the young man again or learned how his interview went, but I assume it went badly. He was approaching hysteria as I left him.

*Accidents happen; don't let them destroy you.*
*Control the damage and get on with your life.*

# Short Way

*Let us be thankful for the fools.*
*But for them, the rest of us could not succeed.*

Mark Twain

Keith, a consulting company sales representative, was frustrated. "Mr. Raymond, all three had great credentials to be your national sales manager. I don't understand."

"What the hell's the matter with you, Keith?" exclaimed the president of the men's clothing distributor. "I'm not talking about credentials! We sell the finest men's suits in America, and my sales manager has to look like it. One guy you sent me was 50 pounds overweight. The other had buttons missing. And the woman, for Christ's sake, she was wearing an evening gown at 8 o'clock in the morning. Sure I want credentials, but my sales manager has to *look sharp!"*

"Yes, sir," replied Keith.

"Good. Now listen. Friday I'll be at the Airport Marriott. There's a conference break at ten. Find me a national sales manager, and bring him to my suite at exactly 10 o'clock. I don't care if it's a man or a woman, but I want to see somebody with *The Look*, understand?"

After three frantic days interviewing people, Keith was about to give up and cancel when he found William: tall, good looking and impeccably dressed, 15 years selling men's clothing, five in management. *All right!* He arranged for them to meet at Mr. Raymond's suite on Friday.

Keith arrived at 9:50 and found Mr. Raymond already there. "Conference broke early. Where's your boy?"

"He'll be here," Keith assured his client. They talked about wrapping up the search that day, and Keith was already spending the consulting fee.

They drank coffee as 10 o'clock came and went. Then 10:10. The phone rang and Mr. Raymond answered it. "It's for you."

Keith's stomach sank. It was William. "I made a wrong turn coming in. I'm in the lobby of the Holiday Inn, and I can see the Marriott from here. It can't be two hundred yards away, but I can't find the right road to get there."

"Okay, look, don't take your car. There's a short way. Go out the front entrance and walk along the service road to your left. It winds around a little, but you'll be here in five minutes."

"No problem," Keith told Mr. Raymond. "He took a wrong turn coming into the airport. He'll be here in five minutes."

**20**

Mr. Raymond glanced at his watch and said nothing. Fifteen minutes later, he grumbled "This is ridiculous. I've got to get back," and got up to leave.

Just then, a knock at the door. "There he is," Keith pleaded. "Please take a few minutes to speak to him. I'm telling you, your job search is over. You won't find anyone else with a look like his."

Keith opened the door wide, and there stood William. Mr. Raymond never had seen anyone look like that. He just stared.

Shoes and trousers up to the knees were soaked and covered in mud, grass stains on his elbows, hair in his face, dripping sweat. A leather attaché case leaked on the carpet.

With a smile, William stepped into the room. "Good morning. I know this is an unusual request at an interview, but do you possibly have a towel I could borrow?"

Curiosity got the better of him, and Mr. Raymond stayed to find out what happened. William dried off and told his story.

"Well, I went out the front entrance and saw a dirt path through the tall grass over toward the Marriott. It looked faster than the road, so I took it. The grass got taller and the ground got spongy and the mosquitoes were biting. I was about to turn back when I slipped and slid down a bank into a ditch half full of muddy water. I couldn't even see the Holiday Inn anymore, but I could see the Marriott so I kept going. And I made it. Here I am."

Without a word, Mr. Raymond got up and left, closing the door with more force than necessary.

Puzzled, William looked at Keith and asked, "Does that mean I don't get the job?"

*A sure thing seldom is and the short way often isn't.*
*Verify directions and destination, and plan enough time*
*to arrive at the interview a few minutes early.*

# Summer Intern

*You might as well fall flat on your face
as to lean over too far backwards.*

James Thurber, 1940

imberley smiled at the silver-haired gentleman as she and her client passed his table.

"Hello, Frank, nice to see you."

Frank didn't even look up. A deep scowl furrowed the face he buried in his menu. He ignored her completely, not a word.

"What was that all about?" Gerry asked, sitting down and unfolding his napkin. "That was bizarre."

"Oh, it's a long story," Kimberley grinned. "It's 23 years now. But I keep hoping."

"I've never seen anything like it. Who is he, a jilted lover? Does he owe you money? What? Come on, you can't just let this one go by."

"It's really a silly story, Gerry, and I'm not particularly proud of it."

"I've got time."

"Let's order first."

When the waiter left, Gerry leaned toward her. "Okay, Kim, my curiosity runneth over. Who is he? *Why* is he?"

And Kimberley began. "Well, you see, it's like this. Twenty-three years ago, I was a summer intern at Frank's bank. He managed the program, hired me, was coach and confessor to us all. 'Just blend in,' he preached. 'Nobody expects you to be a banker. Watch, learn and above all, don't get in the way.'

"I learned a lot that summer, too. It was exciting. I wanted to work for that bank, and interns were practically guaranteed a job after graduation.

"He told us there'd be 'something special' on the last day of the program and to dress up for it. I assumed it'd be some kind of a posh farewell lunch with the brass, you know, the rah-rah stuff. So I skipped breakfast that day and dressed for the executive dining room, it was really frigid in there. I still remember the outfit I wore — long sleeves, high-collared blouse, skirt, jacket, stockings, the whole bit."

"And you were wrong, right?" Gerry sat back as the waiter brought their martinis.

"Yes, I was wrong. We actually went to a groundbreaking in West-chester, a project the bank was financing. We flew up in helicopters to the middle of an open field, no shade at all, just a speaker's platform with chairs for the dignitaries and all us interns, about 300 locals facing us, and it was 96 degrees.

"And the speeches! Well, you know how that goes, they couldn't leave anybody out. The mayor, the senior Republican and Democratic councilmen, the planning commission chairman, the president of the chamber of commerce, the building's owner, the chief tenant, the architect, the general contractor. And the sun beating down all the time. I remember thinking, why do we have to do this in the middle of a field? There's nothing here yet."

Gerry made a sympathetic noise. He'd been through ceremonies like that. "The plot thickens," he said, "what about Frank?"

"Well, about 2 o'clock I was really hungry. My stomach was complaining seriously. I was dehydrating in all those clothes and began to feel faint, just as the president of the bank was speaking. Not a propitious

moment, but I had to get off that platform, find a little shade and some water.

"I remember planning my route — across the platform, behind the speaker, down the stairs. I stood up and began to walk....

"Friends told me later that I got to a point directly behind the president...and fainted, dead away.

"The worst part of it, they said, was that he never even noticed me. The crowd gasped. People stood up, pointing. A couple even rushed forward. And he thought they were getting excited about his speech, a standing ovation. He just kept on talking.

"Now *that's* how to make a bank president remember you! Make him look like a fool! In public! And Frank, well Frank was mortified."

"That's quite a picture," Gerry laughed.

"Anyway, I woke up in an air-conditioned trailer with a construction foreman putting cold, wet paper towels on my forehead. Frank was still there too, I'll give him that. The ceremony was over, the helicopters gone and a car was waiting for us. But the foreman, a man my father's age, wouldn't let me leave until I'd finished a turkey sandwich and two Cokes.

"'She ain't ready yet,' he told Frank, who was trying to hurry me along.

"Well, Frank just shut up and waited. In fact, he didn't say anything during the whole ride back to the city. Or for the next 23 years either! He hasn't forgiven me yet, and probably never will, but I keep trying.

"Anyway, the next day in my exit interview they told me not to worry about it, it could happen to anyone. But I never heard from the bank again, nothing about the incident and no job after I got my degree."

"But no lasting harm," Gerry grinned, "right, Madam Executive Vice President?"

"No, but there could have been. I found out a couple of weeks later that I was pregnant at the time. It could have been a disaster, but everything turned out fine."

"Well, I'm glad to hear that. Now, I understand about Frank, so let's get down to my business. I want your bank to take my company public."

They were in deep discussion when the waiter brought their lunch.

*If you need information, investigate or ask.*

# Planner

*The best laid plans of mice and men*
*are still not as good as a woman's.*

Anonymous

At 25, Cheryl didn't have a college degree, but she'd worked for her cousin as a secretary and made the most of every opportunity to learn. She acquired excellent computer and word processing skills and became an outstanding organizer.

When her cousin made vice president, Cheryl became his executive assistant. That was two years ago, and ever since she'd kept the office running like a Formula 1 racing machine. Cousin Vince had a great mind for theory, she knew, but he couldn't get a single thing done on time without her. She had everything worked out on her calendar, one of those large month-at-a-glance planners that covered almost the entire top of her desk.

Now the time had come to move on. With the nepotism thing, she knew her chances of further advancement were limited. In any case, she needed new challenges. Within a week, she saw a newspaper ad for an executive secretary in a large advertising agency:

> STRONG secretarial and organizational skills; work with senior executives and management committee; maintain schedules, travel arrangements, etc.; oversee office operations.

Perfect, she thought, that's for me, and called the number listed. An appointment was set, and she neatly wrote it down on her desk-top monthly planner, her office bible.

A day or so later, Vince came storming out with a mess of papers in his hand. "Cheryl, where the hell is the back-end of this report and my notes on the Twilling Contract? I haven't got 'em, have you?" He plunked his bottom on her desk, began searching and knocked over her Coke, spilling it all over himself and her sacred planning calendar.

They both cursed. He whipped out a handkerchief to dry his suit. She fumbled for the paper towels in her drawer to blot up the puddles. But the damage was done. The calendar-planner was one big, soggy brown stain full of blurred inky lines. The entries on it were all but illegible. She cursed again.

Cheryl found the papers Vince wanted in his office, then set about cleaning up her desk and reconstructing the calendar. Damn him, she thought. But her anger faded as the day and then the week wore on.

On the day of her interview at the ad agency, Cheryl arrived exactly five minutes early, as was her custom at every meeting. "Good morning," she said cheerfully to the smiling receptionist. "Cheryl Ritter to see Mr. Dupree, please. I have an appointment." The receptionist's smile turned quizzical and she gave Cheryl a strange look. "Well," she said, "I'll see if he's, uh, available and has time to see you. Will you have a seat, please?"

If he's available? thought Cheryl, has time to see me? What's that supposed to mean?

She sat down and browsed through the agency's annual report, and then a brochure presenting its prize-winning ad campaigns. She liked them both. Fifteen minutes passed. She frowned and walked around the reception room, looking at the framed ads. Five more minutes. She went back to the report. Another ten minutes went by. After 45 minutes, Cheryl was about to complain to the receptionist when the inside doors opened. A tall, white-haired man in a plaid suit came over to her.

"Uh, Miss Ritter, is it?" he asked. "How do you do. I'm Mr. Dupree." He didn't invite Cheryl in, but sat down with her in the reception area. Cheryl's brows puckered but she said nothing.

"You do understand, don't you, that the essence of this position is planning and organization?" asked Mr. Dupree.

"Certainly," replied Cheryl with dignity. "Those are my prime qualities. There's nothing I do as well in this world as plan things out carefully ahead of time."

"Interesting," replied Mr. Dupree, stroking his chin. "That's what makes it so odd that we haven't heard from you before now. You see, your interview was scheduled for last Monday."

Oh my God! The Coke, the calendar! I got it wrong!

She tried to explain, but he wasn't buying it, he just seemed amused. When the interview ended, just a few minutes later, Mr. Dupree told Cheryl that the company would be making its decision by the end of the week. On Saturday, Cheryl got the rejection letter — exactly on time.

*Consider keeping copies of critical material in two separate places, just as you back up computer files.*

*Putting job interviews on your desk calendar at work is not the brightest idea either.*

# Taxi

*The actual building of roads devoted to motor cars is not for the
near future, in spite of many rumors to that effect.*

Harper's Weekly, August 2, 1902

Dennis looked at his watch. Almost noon. That's the nice part about looking for a better job in the city, he thought, you can get to an interview at lunch time and be back by 1 pm. He got up to leave.

Oh bloody hell! The boss was headed straight for his desk. "Bill, can I help you?"

"Yeah, Dennis, last month's results look good, but I'd like to know...." He seemed ready to stay a while.

"Gee, Bill, I'm sorry, but can I see you this afternoon? I'm supposed to meet my sister for lunch today."

"Oh, sorry to hold you up. Sure. And listen, next time bring her in so we can all meet her."

"Thanks, I'll do that," Dennis said, rushing out the door and into the elevator. He ran across the lobby and outside to hail a cab. It was raining. Not an empty cab in sight.

"Oh no," he moaned, "not today!"

"Yeah, you and everybody else, buddy," someone behind him growled. "Get in line and wait your turn, huh?"

He turned up his collar and started to walk, hoping to hail a cab along the way. After two blocks, one pulled in to let an old woman out, and he raced three people for it, diving in first.

"Cabbie," he called, leaning forward. "Listen, I have an important meeting to make. There's a ten-dollar tip if you get me there on time."

At first, Dennis wasn't sure if the driver understood. He appeared to be from some Middle Eastern country. Then the taxi lurched forward and weaved in and out of traffic, running red lights, at one point even jumping the sidewalk to get around a double-parked truck.

They were within ten blocks of his interview when the cab stopped short with an awful noise of crunching metal as it plowed into another cab pulling out from the curb. Dennis's head banged into the plexiglass divider, and he could feel a trickle of blood running down his forehead.

The drivers leaped out flailing and screaming at each other in two different languages, neither of them English.

Dennis got out too, and a large man wearing a flowered shirt and blue shorts stepped from the other cab. "Say there, friend, how you doin'? You look a little banged up."

"No, I'm okay, thanks," Dennis replied. "This is a hell of a mess."

"Yeah, well, at least it's stopped rainin'. Say, I'm Big John Jessup, from Oklahoma City. My wife and I are here in the Big Apple on vacation."

"Uh, pleased to meet you, Mr. Jessup," said Dennis. "Look, I don't want to seem rude or anything, but there's this meeting I really have to get to...."

"Oh, you can't leave. You're a witness, like us." Big John grinned, enjoying the excitement. "You might get yourself in a heap o' trouble if you don't stay."

Dennis wasn't sure that was true, but he wasn't sure that it *wasn't* true either. He glanced at his watch. Oh, well, I'm already late, I've got blood on my face and my clothes are wet. I guess I don't have much choice. He spotted a pay phone and called to apologize and reschedule his interview.

It took over a half-hour for two bored police officers to arrive. They separated the cab drivers, took their statements and radioed for tow trucks.

"Are you the passengers?" Dennis and Big John nodded. "Well, you can go." The policemen got back in their prowl car and left before Dennis could say a word.

When he finally got back to the office, he sank gratefully into his chair and booted up the computer. When Bill came by, he had to make up a story about how the cab he and his sister took was in an accident. Then he had to listen to everyone's concern about his sister, which would have been touching except that he didn't have a sister.

Dennis worked late that night to make up for the time he'd missed. At about 6 o'clock, his phone rang. It was the personnel manager he was supposed to see that day.

"Hi, Dennis, I'm glad I caught you. Say, I'm sorry, but I have to cancel your interview next week. We just got word from the top to cut costs. They put a freeze on hiring for at least a year. I hope that doesn't create any problems for you."

"No, not at all," Dennis mumbled. He hung up and decided maybe it was time to go home for the day.

*If you get caught on your way to a clandestine meeting, consider saying "I have an appointment." If they press for details, say "it's personal."*

# Leap of Faith

*Take calculated risks.*
*That is quite different from being rash.*
General George S. Patton, 1944

Perfect Seal Corporation, a small and successful food-packaging company in Seattle, had big plans to break into the more lucrative field of pharmaceutical packaging. Its newly designed machines created airtight, high-strength seals on plastic packaging for liquids and creams, perfect for pharmaceuticals. And Dennis, with his solid drug industry contacts and proven marketing talent, was the man to lead them.

The only problem was that Dennis worked for somebody else.

That didn't stop George, Perfect Seal's president. He'd made contact through a recruiter, and was now waiting for Dennis to arrive. I'll get him, he thought. I'll make him an offer he can't refuse. And the fat, ebullient little man went over his planned sales pitch.

Dennis's initial skepticism began to fade as he listened to George. He couldn't help but react to the man's enthusiasm. George was animated; he couldn't stand still. "We can package more salves, creams and ointments faster, cheaper and with a stronger seal than anybody else in the industry. Come on, I'll show you the prototype line on the floor, see for yourself."

"See that, see that?" George fairly danced around the filling machine. "How's that for a test to prove the system, huh? Grease! We're even putting industrial grease into these poly pouches, and not a trace of external contamination! I tell you, we can package anything. Let's go back to the office, I'll show you actual samples."

Dennis was impressed. More so when he saw the array of packages the secretary had laid out, all with black and gunky grease inside, a pristine package on the outside. "These are great demos at trade shows," George enthused, "total package integrity, even with grease. Here, feel it, feel that." And he tossed a package to Dennis.

"And wait'll you see this!"

George opened a closet and dragged a huge plastic pouch to the middle of the floor. "A special gimmick. I had them make it up for the shows. There's a hundred pounds of grease in there. We get models in bikinis jumping off a ladder into it. The crowd loves it. They actually cheer!"

**31**

Dennis winced. Models in bikinis and a big sack of grease may be great for machinery shows, but not for health care. He cringed at the reaction that would get from doctors.

George, misinterpreting Dennis's frown, got even more excited. "No really, they don't break. Look, I'll show you." And he scrambled up on the desk.

Oh no! Dennis thought. But before he could take cover, George shouted, "They really don't break. Watch!" And he leaped into the center of the grease-filled pouch.

Well, models in bikinis weigh about 90 to 100 pounds. George was 270 at least. Once again, the basic laws of physics proved why they're basic laws.

The pouch exploded! Thick industrial grease splattered over everybody and everything — furniture, walls, ceiling, and of course, Dennis and George.

George sat there on the floor, stunned.

"I'll find my way out," Dennis said in a calm voice.

But George jumped up, put his greased arm around Dennis's spattered shoulders, and walked out the door with him. "A fluke, a fluke, that was only a fluke. I tell you, it's better than sliced bread. With our technology and your marketing know-how, we could take pharmaceutical packaging by storm...." And so he continued as they strolled through the office to the front entrance, ignoring the office people staring after them.

Dennis never did go to work for Perfect Seal. But he heard that the company eventually developed a pouch with a seal so strong even George could jump on it. Apparently, he did it once, too, at a health care trade show, and the doctors loved it.

*Even if an idea is great, you have to be able
to work with your boss to develop it.*

# Hands of Clay

*Shall the clay say to him that fashioneth it, What makest thou?*

Isaiah 45:9

**S**he's beautiful. They all agreed, admiring her.

"Beautiful? She's gorgeous!" Gordon whispered, completely awed as he gazed at her.

And indeed she was — sleek and sexy, low to the ground and fire engine red.

It was the full-sized model of the car that was going to put Ford Motor Company back into the young car buyers' market. People here in the Design Center had spent months developing this next new car "look," and Gordon (Gordo to all) was one of the few outsiders privileged to see her.

Gordo was an engineering job candidate, with excellent academic credentials from the University of Michigan, a preferred hiring source for U.S. car makers. Tall and a little awkward but likable, everyone agreed that he'd be offered a job. The senior engineer, the last to interview him, liked him so much, in fact, that he gave Gordo this special treat, a visit to the Design Center.

In those days, computers were not the all-powerful automotive design tools they are today. Initial car designs were done by computer and artists drew their renderings, but before any company was willing to commit millions to produce a new car they wanted to see it "in the flesh," a full-sized clay model complete in every detail.

The designers build one of these models only when they're very sure they have the final design. The model is expensive and time consuming to craft. It starts with a huge block of clay that is literally sculpted into the shape of the car. All the accessories are included: door handles, mirrors, antenna, nameplate, chrome, paint. Looking at it, anyone would swear it's a real car. Only the glass areas painted in a soft, reflective silver might give it away.

Gordo was awed by both the Design Center and the car. He loved the computers and the drawings and this latest model which had only been completed the night before. The designers were about to start measuring and photographing it from every angle.

On this day, though, there was a problem. No one had told Gordo that he was looking at a clay model.

"Well, what do you think, Gordo?" asked the senior engineer.

"It's beautiful," he replied. "What does the interior look like?"

**34**

Before anyone realized, he tried to open the door. The handle came off in his hand. He lurched backward and instinctively reached out for the side mirror which also ripped off, taking a big chunk of clay with it. As he fell, he grasped at the window molding and gouged the side of the car with his fingers.

Shocked, horrified people began running everywhere and screaming, mostly at Gordo and the senior engineer. The two were escorted out in seconds, none too gently.

Gordo didn't get a job offer from Ford. Rumor had it that the senior engineer was soon looking for another job himself.

Someone got a job out of Gordo's experience, though: a 24-hour security guard to enforce the "Absolutely No Visitors" sign at the Design Center's entrance.

*Some errors can't be fixed. When one happens,*
*chalk it up to experience and learn from your mistake.*

# Quiet Tavern

*How success changes the opinion of men!*
Maria Edgeworth, 1800

Sally, a manufacturer's rep for several medical supply companies, wanted out. Enough of this straight commissions, no insurance, no paid vacation, no pension, she decided. A salaried job in purchasing, that's for me. She wangled a meeting with a distributor, Dr. Peterson of Peterson's Medical Supply.

"Sally, I really don't need another buyer," he told her, "but I tell you what. If you can prove that you'll save money for me, I'll find a way. How's that, fair?"

"Fair enough," she said. "I'll get back to you. And thanks."

She canvassed her industry contacts and learned of a new Korean company looking for business and willing to cut prices to get it. Two principals in the firm were visiting the U.S., and she arranged to meet with them at Dr. Peterson's favorite spot, the taproom of a small, pre-revolutionary inn in the center of the rural Connecticut town.

Arriving early, Sally understood why the local gentry liked the place — low ceilings and pegged floors, a huge fireplace, drinks in pewter mugs, Early Americana throughout. All the leading citizens treated it almost like their own private club. They stopped in every afternoon for a quiet, after-hours drink and a bit of socializing.

Sally was happy to see the Koreans arrive exactly on time, and Dr. Peterson came in soon after. He was a retired physician, about 65, dark suit and tie, soft-spoken, reserved, in a word, dignified. She made the introductions, and they all went to Dr. Peterson's table in the center of the taproom. On the way, he exchanged greetings with virtually everyone there.

"I hope you like it here, gentlemen," said the doctor. "It's an authentic tavern dating back to the 1740s." The Koreans nodded approvingly. They were both about 40 years old. One, whose English was quite good, translated for the other. As far as Sally could tell, they were both named Mr. Kim. "A lovely place, Doctor," said the Mr. Kim who spoke English. Sally had a good feeling.

"Thank you, Mr. Kim. You know, I've gotten to the age where quality of life means much more to me than money. I like to do business in pleasant surroundings."

After the second round of drinks, Sally brought up business. "Korean

**37**

Medical Supply has just begun producing latex examination gloves," she told Dr. Peterson, "and they want to break into the U.S. market." Immediately, the Koreans were all business, drinks put down on the table and calculators at the ready.

"How's your quality?" asked Dr. Peterson.

The Koreans opened one of their two large briefcases and piled boxes of latex gloves on the table, drawing a few curious glances from the other patrons. "Very high quality," said Mr. Kim, as he passed the gloves around.

Dr. Peterson examined them briefly and, without preamble, said, "Thirty dollars a case, minimum buy of 50 cases every two months."

Mr. Kim translated and the two Koreans fell into animated discussion, punching numbers into their calculators. Finally, the Mr. Kim who spoke English said, "Forty dollars, 40 cases every month."

"That's ridiculous, gentlemen," replied the doctor.

That started another heated discussion between the Koreans, louder than before. They were virtually screaming at each other, attracting every eye in the tavern. Dr. Peterson was turning red.

Sally decided to change the subject. "Tell me gentlemen, do you make any other products?"

"Ah, yes," they nodded, and began pulling boxes of condoms from the other briefcase, piling them on top of the gloves. Sally wanted to crawl under the table.

They were the type usually sold from machines in the men's rooms of bars, with glossy pictures of naked women on the packaging. By now, every eye in the tavern focused on their table and Sally heard the waitresses giggling. Please don't open them, she thought to herself.

But the two Mr. Kims already had. One of them pulled out a condom and stretched it wide. "Very high quality, very high."

Sally's heart sank as Dr. Peterson signaled the waitress for the check. He stood up to leave without even saying goodbye. He'd taken two steps when Mr. Kim shouted, "Thirty-five dollars, 60 cases every two months, letter of credit!"

Dr. Peterson came back to the table and shook hands with both Mr. Kims. "Deal, gentlemen. Sally will work out the details. Nice to have met you."

To Sally, "Do you have a word processor at home?"

"Yes I do."

"Good. Write up the contract and bring it in when you start Monday morning. You're my new buyer." Then he leaned down and whispered, "I never really thought I'd get thirty-five. You saved me some money. But next time, let's meet suppliers in the office, okay?"

Despite his "quality of life" talk, Dr. Peterson was a shrewder businessman than he pretended. And for Sally, it would have been a perfect day except that, before they left, the two Mr. Kims passed out samples of their latex gloves and condoms to every patron in the tavern. Sally hasn't had the nerve to go into the place since.

*Anyone can look good when things are going well,*
*but keeping cool when the unexpected occurs can carry the day.*

# Yours If You Want It

*Oh Lord, it is not the sins I have committed that I regret,
but those I have had no opportunity to commit.*

Sheykh Ghalib, 1800

L ou and his wife, Mary, are still happily married after 26 years, three kids...and Leslie.

Lou, a product manager and corporate downsizing victim, met Leslie, a marketing vice president for a Fortune 500 company, at a cocktail party. All evening they talked advertising strategies, product promotions, telemarketing. And Leslie was impressed. "Why don't you call me next week. I might have something you'd be interested in."

"Maybe God really does watch over the deserving unemployed," Lou told Mary at home.

In Leslie's office the next week, they picked up where they'd left off — market shares, competition, pricing. And then, "Lou, let's get down to it. How do you feel about working for a woman?"

"No problem," he assured her.

"Good," and she squeezed his arm. "Incidentally, you're in terrific shape. I like that in my people."

Lou was flattered. The only good part about the past six months was the exercise. At 50, he was trimmer and firmer than he was 25 years ago.

"Let me show you our sales charts." Leslie brushed solidly against him as they moved to the chart wall. Lou noticed, but she didn't seem to. And when they sat down again, Leslie took the chair opposite his. She was animated as she outlined new products in the pipeline, punctuating each one with a familiar slap to Lou's knee.

He was not really sure if she was coming on or he was over-reacting. Women are more demonstrative than men, right? They touch more, don't they?

Then, "You'll have to travel a lot, Lou, any problem there? Are you married?"

"I've always traveled," Lou replied, "and yes I am married. Happily."

"I'm divorced myself," Leslie confided. "I think my career intimidated my husband. I have lots of time for outside activities, if you know what I mean."

Bill Clinton, Clarence Thomas and Bob Packwood, you're not alone, thought Lou.

**40**

He was convinced when Leslie dropped the pencil she was twirling and leaned toward him to pick it up, slowly, eyes never leaving his, her blouse hanging loose, very skimpy bra.

"It's yours if you want it, Lou," she said as she straightened up. "Office is waiting, you can start on Monday."

"Let me sleep on it and I'll call you tomorrow, okay?" They shook hands, and it seemed to Lou that she held on just a little longer than necessary.

Lou told Mary the whole story at dinner that night, and she thought it was funny. "Poor baby. And what were you doing looking down her blouse anyway?"

"Don't laugh, she was coming on to me," he said indignantly. "I was embarrassed."

Mary was still amused. "Sure she was, honey. The shoe pinches on the other foot, doesn't it."

Lou turned Leslie down and eventually did get another job.

*If it's clear that sex, or another "extra," is an important part of the job and you don't want it, decline the offer.*

# Oil Baron

*What a mad idea to demand equality for women! Women are nothing but machines for producing children.*

Napoleon Bonaparte (1769-1821)

**O**il, Black Gold, fascinated Susan. She wanted to be part of that industry, but she knew she had two major handicaps. She'd be a woman in a man's industry, and she was a Northerner, when all the action was down South.

But she was also smart and determined. She moved to Louisiana, got an analyst's job with a Fortune 500 oil company there and soon earned a reputation. She knew everything from regional rig counts, reserves and production to global market shares, demand and prices. Her boss had little Post-It notes printed up: "Check with Susan."

She learned quickly how to deal with the "good old boys" too: be direct, look 'em right in the eye. She could walk into a meeting and give a handshake as firm as any man's. She carried an attaché case, and wore clothes to mask her femininity. God help the man who called her "little lady."

Despite her success in the *business* of oil, Susan wanted to get into the real heart of the industry – *drilling.* When she heard that a well-known independent producer had an opening, she pestered its president until he agreed to see her. She'd really have to sell herself, and she knew it.

Susan walked into their headquarters office and shuddered. It was going to be even tougher than she'd thought. The only women here were secretaries, and they all had figures like a Playboy Playmate.

"Hi, honey," said the busty blond at the reception desk. "How can ah he'p y'all?"

Susan gritted her teeth and smiled. "I'm Susan Slade, and I have an appointment with Mr. Latham about the vice president's position."

"Oh my," the blond declared, her big blue eyes going wide. "Well, now, y'all jus' set yose'f down an' ah'll go tell Mr. Latham yoah heah." She swayed out of the room on spike heels. Oh brother! thought Susan.

Ten minutes later she was ushered into a huge office. Behind the gleaming cherrywood desk was Mr. Latham, about 50 years old, big and leathery. She gave him her firmest handshake and looked him in the eye. He wasted no time getting to the point.

"Now, ah know yo' got a good li'l reputation theah, Suzy, but ah need somebody to really take cha'ge. Drillers are a tough bunch a bastards — sorry, ah meant guys — and ah'm just not sure a gal can han'le 'em. Hell, mos' *men* can't han'le 'em."

Male chauvinist pig, she thought. But she'd heard it all before and had her stock answer ready: people stop worrying about my sex the minute I start making money for them.

This time, though, she thought she'd better emphasize to Latham that she could be "one of the boys" too. She strode over to the desk and plunked herself solidly on the corner, ready to show him all the profit numbers up close, eye to eye.

But as she swung her attaché case up, the latch popped and dumped everything on his desk...including a purse-size box of Tampax. It skidded right under his nose.

Latham turned the same deep red as his cherrywood desk.

"Excuse me," she said quickly, scooping everything back into the case. "Now, where were we? Right, profits."

She tried to continue, but the interview was effectively over. She'd lost him. He just sat there, still red, fidgeting in his seat and looking uncomfortable, obviously hoping she'd leave.

Susan didn't get the job. She still works in the oil industry, but on the business side. She wondered, though: if that latch hadn't broken....

*When you travel, make sure your bags
and briefcase are securely fastened.*

# Natural Order

*If men cannot cope with women in the medical profession,*
*let them take a humble occupation in which they can.*

Emma Hart Williar in an 1853 editorial
in the women's magazine *Godey's Lady Book*

**D**octors? On job interviews? Yeah, sure, when pigs don't snort and Rodney Dangerfield gets some respect. That's the common impression.

But doctors do interview. It happens all the time, especially today with so many group medical practices. Group practice is becoming the norm and usually requires unanimous approval of a new member by *all* physicians in the group. That means a whole *series* of interviews.

Take Robin, for instance. She'd completed her residency in obstetrics and gynecology at Duke University Medical Center in Durham — a Duke woman all the way, undergraduate and medical degrees, internship and residency. All told, she'd been in North Carolina for 11 years and loved it, a true transplant from Long Island.

Robin hoped to get into a group practice in nearby Chapel Hill. They needed an OBG person, and she'd already met successfully with five of the group's six doctors, all men. Last came "Old Doctor Stern," as the others referred to him, the senior partner who had started the group. His vote was "a lot more equal" than theirs.

Dr. Stern was about 70, tall, angular, with a blunt, no-nonsense manner. They sat in his office with the door closed. After a perfunctory greeting, he stroked his Van Dyke, looked directly into her eyes for a long moment and asked, "Doctor, what makes you want to join this particular practice?"

"Many reasons, Dr. Stern," she said. "I like and respect all the doctors here. The group has a very solid reputation. There's a need for OBG specialists in Chapel Hill, with all the graduate students and young research people in 'The Triangle' and all. You have an opening. And I think I could add something to the practice by bringing in a woman's point of view."

"Really? Why would a woman's point of view add anything?" asked Dr. Stern, surprised.

"Well, gynecological problems are very personal to a woman. She may be embarrassed discussing them and being examined by a man. She might prefer talking to a woman who knows how she feels."

**44**

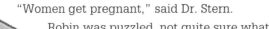

"Women get pregnant," said Dr. Stern.

Robin was puzzled, not quite sure what he meant. "Well, yes, certainly, they do, and I'm equally interested in the obstetrical side of the practice."

"No, no, you miss my point," said old Dr. Stern impatiently. "I have never brought a woman into the practice. Physician or not, a woman will want to get married, have babies and stay home. It's the natural order of things. Frankly, when I first saw your name, I thought you were a man. Your credentials are excellent, but if I'd known, I wouldn't have agreed even to interview you."

Robin was stunned. What century is this man living in? "There are thousands of successful women doctors who are married and raising families too, equally successfully," she said, more than a little annoyed. "Besides, I don't even have a boyfriend."

"Well, eventually you'll get one. Then you'll get married, have a baby and want to leave the practice," announced Dr. Stern with absolute certainty. "I'm sorry, doctor, but we'll be investing too much in you even to take a chance. But thank you for coming in."

The physician in Robin wondered seriously if Dr. Stern was in early stages of Alzheimer's; she wished she could do some tests. Her feminist side wondered if the world had stopped for him thirty years ago. There was no point in arguing, so she thanked him for his time and left.

Telling the story later to her friend Judy, also a doctor, she was still incensed. Judy advised her to sue for blatant discrimination. "No, I don't want to sue my way into a practice. I want to be welcome, a member of the team, not someone forced on them by a bunch of lawyers."

Robin did join another group in nearby Raleigh and was happy there. She kept her eye on Dr. Stern's practice, though, just out of curiosity. Two years later Dr. Stern retired, and a week after that, the group brought in its first female gynecologist.

*Whether you choose to fight discrimination or forget it,*
*your first priority is to stay focused on finding a job.*

# Perfect Couple

*She shall be called Woman, because she was taken out of Man.*

Genesis 2:18

**Y**ou could almost feel the résumé writer blushing over the telephone.

"How do you change genders on the SF-171* software?" she asked headquarters in almost a whisper.

"What? I don't know, I'd have to look it up. Why, for God's sake?"

"I did a 171 for a woman six months ago and she just called for a redo," the writer explained. "She and her husband both had sex change operations — she is now he and he is she; Samantha is Sam and Robert is Roberta. And they're still married! How do they do that?"

Headquarters walked her through the software procedure to change genders, but not the surgical procedure.

*You are who you are, and if others have a problem with that, it's their problem, not yours.*

---

*SF-171, for Standard Form 171, is the U.S. Government's standard employment application, available as a paper form and as a software package.

# Get Off My Cloud[*]

*The more I see of men, the more I admire dogs.*

Jeanne-Marie Roland (1754-1793)

**V**inny and Augie lounged with styrofoam coffee cups at their customary 9 am post, the intersection of two major 33rd-floor corridors, admiring the flow of women arriving for work. It was a particularly good day, with temperature and humidity both headed for three digits and all the women dressed for it — minimally.

"Hey Vinny, who the hell is *that*?"

They watched Victoria MacLoed approaching. Tall, blond, blue eyes, hourglass figure. She gave them a disdainful glance as she floated past, chatting in a delightful British accent about computer languages to John Berger, a mid-level software development manager. They went into the conference room.

"He's gonna *interview* her, Vinny."

"If that nerd turns her down, I'll *whack* him!" Vinny sounded serious.

They sauntered down the corridor and took up a new position, trying to look casual by the conference room door, ears to the paneling.

"So, Miss *Macloyd*, how much experience do you have developing MVS COBOL systems?"

"Rather more than five years, Mr. Berger. And my name is pronounced Mycloud, not *Macloyd*. Victoria *Mycloud*, but please call me Victoria."

Her British accent was incredibly sexy. Augie's spontaneous, low-volume rendition of the Rolling Stones classic "*Get Off My Cloud*" ended in such a fit of suppressed giggles they both nearly spilled their coffee. Ears back to the door.

"So, Victoria, how would you tell if a binary field with a PIC clause of S9(4) COMP is positive or negative?"

Vinny squeezed his eyes shut and prayed, "C'mon, babe, tell 'im. It's the high-order bit. Tell the nerd about the high-order bit."

"One must examine the bit in the high-order position of the field. If it is *on*, the field is negative and the number is carried in two's complement form. If it is *off*, the field is positive and the number is carried in normal form."

---

*Song title by Mick Jagger and Keith Richards.

"*YES!*" Augie and Vinny exchanged "high fives." They pressed their ears back to the door, but too hard and the door flew inward. Both tumbled into the conference room, Vinny going down at Miss *Mycloud's* feet and Augie spilling his coffee.

Berger was cool. "Pay no attention to them, Victoria, they're only operators. Let's find another conference room where it's dry and more private."

Victoria showed no reaction as she stepped around the two young men.

Victoria MacLoed got the job and eventually became assistant vice president for information services.

Vinny and Augie still refer to her, privately, as *Get-Off*. She good-naturedly calls them *Bloody Sods*.

*Today's candidate could be tomorrow's boss.*

**49**

# Picket Line

*I can hire one half of the working class to kill the other half.*

Jay Gould

Twenty-two years old, petite and pretty, with a new engineering degree, Mary wanted to be an automotive production engineer and *make* something. No "token female" staff job for her!

The trouble was, nobody hired women for those jobs in 1968. Except Michigan Brake Parts. They called her in to talk about an operations job on the plant floor. And park in the shopping center across the street, they told her, it'll be easier.

When she arrived, she realized why. A full-fledged strike was in progress: police cars and helmeted cops with night sticks, an angry picket line, inflammatory signs, bullhorns blaring obscenities at the company. A delivery van at the gate was being mobbed by strikers trying to tip it over.

Wonderful! she thought. Why didn't they tell me? Is this some kind of test to see if I can get inside? Engineers have to cross that line every day. Okay, if that's what they want, I'll show 'em, I'll get inside!

In the shopping center she bought a pen and small notepad, then strode right to the center of the action at the main gate.

"Who's in charge here? I'm from the *Detroit Free Press*, covering the strike. I want to ask a few questions before I go in and talk to management." The union guys were happy to list their demands, and then cleared a path for her through the gate.

Mary walked into the plant.

Inside, she was an instant celebrity. The office people all wanted to hear her story and tell their own about how they crossed "The Line." She was accepted immediately, caught up in the general excitement, the camaraderie of sharing a common experience.

When she finally got to her interview, it went well. Even the company president wanted to see her, to hear how she got through the picket line. He loved it.

"Clever, very clever," he admired. "An engineer who can handle production people. I want that around here," and he offered Mary a job on the spot.

She accepted and became the first woman in the company, maybe in the industry, to be just "an engineer," not "a female engineer."

*When confronted by an obstacle, don't give up.*
*Take a breath and consider your alternatives.*
*Ingenuity and tenacity can pay off.*

# Cocktail Waitress

*Morality, like beauty, is in the eye of the beholder.*
Anonymous

*Roy was the new assistant personnel manager of a large hotel in Boston, assigned to hire a cocktail waitress for the lounge.*

"Hot damn! I have to hire a beautiful woman. Who'll wear *this*. And *I'll* get paid for it. Best assignment of my life. Maybe I'll interview a dozen of 'em."

An ad in all the local college newspapers brought a flood of responses, and I rubbed my hands in anticipation. Roy, it doesn't get any better than this, I happily told myself.

When the first girl came in, I was grinning through my professional face. We talked a while, and I showed her the skimpy little outfit she'd have to wear. "No way!" she huffed, and stalked out. Oh well, I thought, there's lots more where she came from.

There were, too. Beautiful young college girls came in one after another ... and stormed out one after another when I showed them the shiny little costume. "Male chauvinist sexist pig," I heard more than once, even though it was actually less revealing than a bikini. I was discovering that Boston is much more conservative than New York where I worked before. My dream assignment was turning into a nightmare. It had me grinding my teeth.

Then Angela walked in. Face, figure — gorgeous! Poised and friendly, too. *Plus* two years of waitressing experience. I was scared to death to show her the outfit, but finally I had to.

"No problem," she said, and *she* was grinning at *me*, at my obvious discomfort.

"Look," she said, fumbling in her large tote. She pulled out a well-known men's magazine, opened it to the "Girls of Summer" photo essay and pushed it at me. "That's me!" she said proudly, pointing at the full-page, totally nude picture of her playing volleyball. "It's this month's issue. That waitress outfit's no problem," she assured me.

I was delighted to have filled the job, but a little disappointed that my search was over. I told Angela the job was hers as far as I was concerned, but I had to clear it with the hotel manager. I'd call her that afternoon.

**52**

"Absolutely not!" the manager barked when I told him about Angela.

"Well, why not?"

"Because this is a conservative Boston hotel. We're not going to have a nude model working here. Let her get a job at one of those topless places in the Combat Zone [Boston's notorious red light district], but not here." He was unequivocal.

I was peeved. "Isn't it a little hypocritical to tell a girl she has to wear that tiny little outfit, and then refuse to hire her for showing a bit more?"

He just shook his head and walked away. Then he turned and said with the hint of a smile, "Welcome to Boston, Roy. You'll get used to it."

The hotel's male employees weren't so conservative. Word about Angela spread, and by the end of the day the lobby newsstand was sold out of that magazine, from under the counter of course.

*Consider the culture of the organization before you reveal too much about your background. Some skills are less transferable than others.*

# Hot Offer

*Make your employers understand that you*
*are in their service as workers, not as women.*

The Revolution, October 8, 1868
Women's suffrage newspaper

**E**velyn was not comfortable with the way the interview for the secretary's job was going. The interviewer looked her over too closely when she sat down, especially when she crossed her legs. His constant grin was lecherous. He gave her a too familiar, exaggerated wink when he said there'd be lots of "evening work." He never even asked about her secretarial skills. And he was offering $5,000 over the normal salary range. She put it all together.

"You don't want a secretary," she spat out, "and *I'm* not giving what you *do* want!"

She reported her experience in detail to the referring employment agency, and raised holy hell when the agency manager told her four other women had turned that job down for what he had felt were flimsy reasons.

"Why didn't you tell me that, or at least warn me!" she chastised. "Well, what are you gonna do about it?" she pushed, "keep sending women over there? Give him his jollies?"

The agent tore up the client company's file card in front of Evelyn.

He later sent her to a utility company where she worked for 20 years.

*Be candid with your employment counselor*
*about your experience at the interview.*

# His Better Half

*The prolonged slavery of women*
*is the darkest page in human history.*

Elizabeth Cady Stanton (1815-1902)

They were a modern career couple. Jill earned $80,000 at a New York investment company; Ray made $50,000 at a small accounting firm. Jill was offered a promotion to Boca Raton at $95,000.

"It's a no-brainer, Jill, take it. I'm not hung up on all this macho stuff. Besides, I can work anywhere, and all I have to make is 35 to keep us even, with sun and palm trees to boot. Take it." She leaned over and kissed him.

Six months later, in a new house and beautiful weather, Jill was prospering and Ray was jobless.

Not that people weren't interested. He'd been on interviews, all right, but they all went the same way. "Sounds good, Ray. Tell me, what brought you down here from New York?" He'd explain about his wife's promotion...and get *The Look,* a quizzical stare that told him exactly how the interviewer felt. A real man doesn't give up a job to follow his wife, ergo he must be a wimp. Nobody ever came out and said it, but the ensuing conversations were always awkward and short.

What irked him most was that the supposedly liberated women he talked with had exactly the same attitude. One personnel manager even gave a little sneer and said, "Well, well, isn't that a switch." Ray wanted to reach across and smack her. The hypocrisy of it all!

Would he ever work again? How many days could he kill at the mall? The average age of the men he saw there was about 80 anyway.

Depression set in with a vengeance. Maybe if I wait long enough, he thought, I can say I came here to retire.

He finally pulled himself out of his funk and decided to take another approach.

At his next interview, at a small accounting firm about the size of the one he'd left in New York, he was talking with the senior partner when the question came.

"So tell me, Ray, why did you leave New York for Boca?"

"Well, Ferris, the truth is, my firm was letting people go and I was worried. With the recession and all, their business was heading south and

**55**

I thought maybe I should too, you know, go where the action is. Besides, my wife always wanted to live in Florida."

"Ray, I hear that from people all the time. You don't have to worry about us though. We're solid as a rock. How about kids? Does your wife work?"

Ray was ready for those standard but illegal questions too. With a proud smile, he answered, "No, Jill is a housewife. No kids yet, but now that we're out of New York, it's time. Jill wants a bunch of 'em. She's the domestic type, if you know what I mean."

"That's great," Ferris said warmly. "It's a wonderful place to raise kids. Ray, I think you're going to fit in real well here."

◎

*Be prepared for "why" questions:*
*"Why did you leave your last job?"*
*"Why do you want this job?"*
*"Why did you move here?"*
*This is not small talk.*
*Plan your answers carefully.*

# Svelte

*If ladies be but young and fair, they have the means to know it.*

William Shakespeare, *As You Like It*

Laura, 30 and attractive, hustled directly from her regular lunch-hour workout to her 2 o'clock interview and quickly sensed why the personnel manager's position was vacant.

George, the division president, middle-aged and overweight, immediately turned the conversation toward hiring practices.

"How do you feel about hiring disabled people, Laura, especially the ones in, you know, wheelchairs?"

She assumed he was testing her. "I'm totally committed to barrier-free workplaces and hiring the handicapped," she replied truthfully. "In fact, two people in wheelchairs work out regularly at the same club I go to. They're impressive people."

"Really?" George sounded surprised. "I like to avoid hiring those people. If they don't work out, they're almost impossible to get rid of. And to tell you the truth, they make me uncomfortable. I'd rather be around normal people all day."

Laura took a deep breath. Maybe he just needs a little educating.

"George, as your potential personnel manager, I have to tell you. You cannot legally discriminate against the handicapped. They're real people, like us. Those two guys in wheelchairs I work out with? Talk to either one a few minutes and you forget the wheelchair."

George ogled as she talked. "You know, I could tell you work out. You have absolutely beautiful legs."

Incredible, Laura thought. A few racial slurs and he'll make the *Guinness Book of Records* for illegal comments in a single interview. Cool down and decide how to play it, Laura. Take a few minutes.

She said, "I, uh, I think I'd like to use the Ladies Room."

"Certainly," George replied. "It's just down the hall. I'll show you." He went with her.

Inside, she decided to leave, just walk out, not even go back to George's office. But when she opened the door, there he was, standing guard.

"I wouldn't want a beautiful woman like you to get lost on the way back," he said with what she supposed he meant as a charming smile.

Hesitant, she went with him and George babbled on about the position, the company, the marketplace...ogling her all the time.

"Look, I'm sorry," she said after a few minutes of that. "I have another appointment. I have to leave." And she did. Quickly.

She drove back to the gym, seriously considering a sexual harassment suit against George, and went straight to the Stairmaster to work off steam.

"Yo, Laura," called Sylvia. "What're you doing back? I thought you had an interview."

"I did."

"Did they want you for the position?"

"Yeah, the missionary position!"

She never did hear from George.

◎

*Evaluate your potential employer as he evaluates you.*
*If you don't like what you see, walk away.*

# The Way We Were

*Lovers' quarrels are the renewal of love.*

Publius Terentius Afer (190-159 BC)

It was harder for Gary when the big layoff came. He still didn't have his life together after a long and bitter divorce, and now this. Everything was headed downhill.

Resigned, he put a résumé together and papered the country with it. Nothing. The recession was in full swing. It figures, he moped.

Finally, after weeks, he got an interview with a local company and spent two days psyching up for it.

Standing tall again, he arrived 15 minutes early and connected right away with the human resources guy. They talked easily. Gary's background fit their needs to a "T." The sun came out again.

"We usually ask people back," the manager told him, "but if you've got time, I'd like you to see a couple of people today. They haven't seen your résumé, but just hand 'em one, okay?"

"Okay!" Gary answered. "I've got all afternoon."

The manager made a call and walked Gary down the hall into a large, windowed and carpeted office. A tall woman sat behind an imposing mahogany desk, her back to them, talking on the phone.

The voice! Gary's heart stopped.

Swinging around, she saw them. And froze.

A long moment later, "Hello, Gary."

"Hello, Sally."

"Uh, you two know each other?" the human resources manager mumbled.

"We were married for eight years," Gary said softly.

"Uh, great," the manager said, obviously embarrassed. "Then you'll have a lot to talk about." He backed out of the room and shut the door. Gary could have killed him.

The conversation wasn't as bad as it could have been. After two years, they found they could be civil to each other. It was childish, he knew, but it bothered him tremendously to be sitting there out of work while his ex-wife was obviously prospering. He did appreciate the fact that she didn't gloat.

"I'm sorry you got laid off, Gary."

"It was the whole department, really. Jeff Wendell might even lose his house."

"That's terrible. Listen, Gary, despite what went on between us, I'd never try to embarrass you like this. He didn't tell me your name, just that he had a good candidate I should see."

"It's okay, Sally, not your fault," he said, deflated and resigned again. The wounds were older but not yet healed.

She walked him to the door and gave him a business-like handshake and one of her cards. It felt odd to touch her hand again.

Gary eventually got another job, but Sally's business card sat on his kitchen table for a long time. In case I ever need a networking contact, he told himself, you know, just business, that's all.

*Before an interview, ask for the names, titles*
*and functions of the people you'll be talking with.*

*Then follow up with a thank-you note.*

# Déjà Vu

*A man is as old as he feels, a woman is as old as she looks.*

French expression

**B**eautiful, competent secretaries learn early about unwanted advances by middle-aged bosses. Sharon had. But in this job she was lucky. Mr. Kessler, a perfect gentleman in his mid-50s, had hired Sharon three weeks earlier on a month's probation. She was sure she'd get the job. Only another week to make it permanent.

On that Friday at 5 o'clock, in swept a voluptuous young woman in her early 20s — expensively dressed and jingling with jewelry. "I'm Mrs. Kessler," she announced, eying Sharon closely, and proceeded into her husband's office.

Two minutes later, Mr. and Mrs. Kessler left. On the way out, she gave Sharon a look that can only be described as venomous.

On Monday morning Mr. Kessler told Sharon, with obvious embarrassment but no explanation, that he wouldn't be hiring her permanently.

Shaken and thoroughly upset, she fought back the tears until she reached the ladies room. Two of the other girls followed her.

"Don't take it so hard, Sharon," they soothed. "It was inevitable. We all knew you didn't have a chance for that job the day you walked in."

"But why? I was doing so well!"

"Absolutely nothing to do with it, Sharon. You just look too good."

"What? What do you mean?"

"Mr. Kessler used to be married to a wonderful woman his own age — three kids, house in the country, the whole bit. Then he hired this young girl as his secretary, and the next thing, they're having an affair, he gets divorced and the secretary is the new Mrs. Kessler."

"The one on Friday?"

"Right. She comes in every couple of weeks to check out the new girls. I guess she figures if he did it once, he'd do it again."

Sharon picked up her final paycheck the next week from Mr. Kessler's new secretary — a woman about 70.

*Performance is not always the issue*
*when you lose or don't get a job. Move on.*

Chapter 3

# Other Side
## of the
# Desk

# The Dump

*The rain to the wind said,*
*"you push and I'll pelt."*
*They so smote the garden bed*
*That the flowers actually knelt*
*And lay lodged, though not dead.*
*I know how the flowers felt.*

Robert Frost, "Lodged"

*Paul was director of technical support for a large com-*
*puter project in New York City employing over 150 con-*
*sultants and looking for more.*

It was 8 am Monday in midtown Manhattan, early February with gray skies leaking a steady drizzle, and I was wondering if this really was the worst hangover I ever had. I rode up in the elevator with 20 other "suits" who didn't want to be there either, and finally slumped into my naugahyde chair.

"Oh, we do need our coffee this morning, don't we?" Glo greeted me. She's my executive assistant, and I like her — smart and tough, not one of those feminine females, if you know what I mean.

She was humming "Oh What a Beautiful Morning" as she set a large mug of black coffee on my desk. "Here's your fix, boss. And to help you feel better, there was an S0C4 abend* on one of the CICS transactions during system test last night. The dump's on your credenza and the boss wants an answer...NOW!"

There it was, all right, a hex-dump a foot-and-a-half thick! "And don't forget," Glo added with sympathy I could almost believe was real, "you have an 8:30 interview. Rosalie's bringing her over, supposed to be a genuine whiz kid with CICS/COBOL." My stomach turned. I wasn't sure I could handle Rosalie and another of her brain-children this morning.

"Cancel it." But I was too late. Rosalie was already in the door with the candidate, I'll call her Corky, and in they came, spouting banalities — what an exciting project, the forefront of the information superhighway, this project really needs a CICS/COBOL expert.

---

* An S0C4 abend is a program ending abnormally (**ab**normal **end**ing) with a mainframe memory violation considered dangerous to the operating system. When an S0C4 abend occurs, the operating system terminates the program and generates a dump — a hexadecimal printout of the computer's memory used for debugging.

Glo retreated but left the door open. There was an excellent chance that a classic encounter of the worst kind was shaping up here. My headache got worse.

"Do you have a current résu..."

"Of course! Of course!" Rosalie jumped in, almost skipping to my desk. "Here's Corky's résumé. She's a *magna* in Computer Science from Binghamton. Look at it, Paul. This project needs her. In fact, from what I hear, you can't succeed without her."

I looked at the résumé and then at Corky. "How much actual experience do you have working on large commercial projects in a CICS/COBOL environment?" I asked.

"Oh, does that really matter?" Corky asked dismissively. "I studied all about it in school and got straight As. Remember, I'm a *magna* from Binghamton!" Rosalie smiled broadly as she watched Corky taking control of the situation.

And the evil that lurks in every man came alive in me. I couldn't help it, it just wouldn't be denied.

"Can you solve S0C4s?" I asked quietly. Rosalie, at least, should have noticed the change as I leaned back and laced my hands behind my head. But she didn't. And neither of them saw Glo's head peek around the door.

"I don't think there'll ever be a computer problem I can't solve," Corky gushed. "Other people, yes, but they could never stump me at school. I solved everything they gave me, and I used to help all my classmates, too."

With that, I got up and walked slowly to the credenza, picked up the dump and held it in front of Corky's face...then SLAMMED it down on the desk in front of her.

WHAAACK! Like Rocky Balboa's left hook landing in Apollo Creed's midsection.

Corky jumped. Rosalie looked sick. And I leaned over and fairly snarled at Corky, "Solve this one!"

She looked up at me, eyes wide. Then down at the dump. Then back at me. And burst into tears. Totally lost it.

Glo winked as she gently put her arm around Corky and led her from the office. Rosalie glared at me and stormed out behind them.

The devil made me do it, I grinned. I still didn't feel good, but I felt better as I sat down to wade into that dump.

*If you tell a hiring manager in a technical interview*
*that you're the best he's ever seen and his mega-project*
*can't succeed without you, be prepared to back it up.*

**65**

# Drip

*I never forget a face, but I am willing to
make an exception in your case.*

Groucho Marx

There I was, sitting behind my polished oak desk, staring at the drip. What had started as a normal interview was turning into water torture.

As a technical manager for AT&T, I was interviewing candidates for a technical support position. This one started out like all the others but went downhill, literally, from there.

The candidate, Sam, introduced himself with a hearty handshake. He had all the requisites: a Ph.D. with relevant and successful work experience. He also seemed intense, highly focused and undeniably enthusiastic, even animated.

The only problem was...the drip.

As Sam began to tell me about his last job, I noticed a small bubble of saliva form in the corner of his mouth. It was not too distracting, just there. Then, as he went on, it grew larger. And larger. I watched.

The bubbles became a drip. The drip gained critical mass. And slowly, it began to ooze down his chin.

I tried to concentrate on what Sam was saying, but my attention riveted on the drip. I wiped my own chin, hoping he'd get the hint. He didn't.

When he came to the major achievement of his last job, nodding vigorously, the drip quickened its southward journey until it finally came to rest on the very tip of his chin. By this time, I was a little disgusted but fascinated nonetheless. How long would this play out?

Forever it seemed. It just stayed there. No matter how animated his conversation, the drip clung to the tip of his chin. And I watched. I should probably have simply told him about it, but now I'd waited too long.

I leaned back in my chair and again tried to concentrate on what he was telling me. I tried to listen, I really did, but... that drip. Why doesn't it just fall off and be done with it? It was defying all laws of physics, hanging there, swaying.

Finally, I ended the interview. Sam stood up and leaned forward to hand me an extra copy of his résumé when...it fell. Splat. On the résumé. An inch away from my thumb. It completely obliterated his "Education."

Yuck! It was no longer fascinating. In fact, it was all I could do to hold on to that paper.

I didn't hire Sam, mainly because all I could remember about him was ... the drip.

*By the time you get to the interview, your credentials, background and experience have already passed review. Hiring managers are also looking for compatibility. Subtle things like body language, tone of voice, personality, even leisure activities can sway judgments. Little things that, by themselves, would not make a difference can add up to a "no."*

**67**

# Screener

*By working faithfully eight hours a day,
you may eventually get to be a boss
and work twelve hours a day.*

Robert Frost

I was only a few years out of school when I was made production manager at the small metal fabricating company I worked for in Connecticut. "David," the owner told me, "I have full confidence in you, but you'll need help with the paperwork. Hire an administrative assistant."

We had no Personnel Department, but we had Mrs. Miller. Nobody really knew how long she'd been there or what she did. Mostly, it seemed, she made good coffee, brought in cake and cookies for birthdays and sympathized with everybody's personal problems. She offered to handle the search for me, but I was leery. I was sure I could do better myself.

So I put an ad in the *Stamford Advocate* and the résumés flooded in. When Mrs. Miller brought my coffee on the day I set aside for interviewing (she insisted on bringing coffee to all "her boys"), she asked very sincerely, "David, can I help you? I'd be happy to talk with them first, screen them for you and save you some time."

"Thanks, Mrs. Miller," I said, "but I really think I'd like to meet them all myself, you know, get a complete picture, form my own opinions. I appreciate the offer though."

"Well, okay," she said, "but if you run into any problems, dear, just pick up the phone and call me."

After the first three, I was getting the hang of it, even wrapping them up quickly. And when Melissa failed to show for her 11:30 appointment, I didn't mind. I could use the time. So I ordered in a sandwich and got to work on next week's production schedule. The next candidate wasn't due until 1 pm.

Melissa finally did show up at 12:45. I knew right away that I wouldn't hire her — she offered no explanation for being late — but it was easier and kinder to talk with her a few minutes. She spoke in a whisper, produced word processing course completion "certificates" on plain paper with no dates or schools listed and mostly stared at her feet. A few minutes before one, I decided I'd been kind enough. I said, "Thanks for coming in, Melissa, you'll hear from me one way or another by next week," and extended my hand.

She didn't move. Still staring at her feet, she whispered, "I know you won't give me the job. I get dressed up, come to all these interviews, show my certificates and they don't hire me. It's because I'm black."

And she started to cry. Softly at first and then in huge gasps, sobs louder than anything she'd said during the interview.

There I stood: my first month in a new job...the owner trusted me and my judgment...alone in my office with the door shut...a timid young woman crying hysterically. Besides having no clue what to do, I was petrified. Every discrimination and sexual harassment headline I'd ever read flashed through my mind. And the 1 o'clock appointment was just outside.

I was afraid to touch Melissa and try to calm her down, even to get close to her, and she showed no signs of stopping. In desperation, I dialed Mrs. Miller. "Would you come in for a minute, please? I have a little situation here. I could use your help."

Mrs. Miller arrived immediately, to my extreme relief. With a lot of "you poor thing ... there, there, dear, things will get better" and sympathetic hugs, she quieted Melissa and soon ushered her out of the building to her car in the lot.

But I was completely unnerved. I just couldn't face another interview that day, so I asked Mrs. Miller to talk to the others and retreated into my office.

I came in early the next morning, made the coffee and personally delivered a cup to Mrs. Miller with my heartfelt thanks. She eventually narrowed the choice to two highly qualified candidates, and then I did select my own administrative assistant.

*Delegating to a capable associate optimizes your time and resources.*

# Open House

*Neither snow, nor rain, nor heat, nor gloom of night stays these couriers from the swift completion of their appointed rounds.*

Inscription on the General Post Office, New York City

*Lo, the big-city bicycle messenger, a breed unto himself: peerless, fearless and tireless. Not traffic lights or predatory taxicabs, one-way streets or old ladies in crosswalks slow him from the swift completion of **his** appointed rounds. After all, he's paid by the number of documents he delivers.*

In today's world of telephone and fax, e-mail, computer networks and FedEx, low-tech bicycle messengers still thrive in major cities, providing their own form of instant communication.

Law firms, financial institutions, printers and others rely on these couriers to deliver confidential and time-is-of-the-essence documents within the hour. These usually scruffy, always aggressive young men swarm untamed over clogged streets and sidewalks on their stripped-down bikes — our urban equivalent of the fabled Pony Express.

And Kathleen recognized their worth.

As administration manager at a large law firm in downtown Manhattan, Kathleen knew she needed the bicycle messengers. But she didn't like the firm's legal paper flying around the city in the backpack of some unknown. She insisted on hiring the firm's own messenger, fully vetted and bonded, for their clients' added protection and confidentiality. The managing partner approved.

Kathleen booked a room at a prestigious hotel in the downtown financial district and placed an ad in *The Village Voice:*

> WANTED – reliable bicycle messenger; salary + overtime, medical benefits, paid vacation. Apply Conference Room G, Grande Hotel, Thursday, 8/26, 12 noon to 3 pm.

A job made in Heaven for the messenger!

At the appointed hour, 400 young men in sweaty T-shirts and no shirts, ragged cut-offs and filthy sneakers, descended on the posh hotel. They pushed, shoved and shouted at each other in Spanish, Greek, Arabic and a few other languages.

Kathleen was stunned. The hotel's day manager was decidedly unhappy. The security staff massed.

They moved Kathleen's casting call into a large ballroom to get the messengers out of the lobby. While she interviewed at one end, the crowd discovered the three telephones at the other. Room service carts began to appear, and the hotel bill later itemized calls to Bogotá and Medellín, Athens, Port Said, Cairo and Charleston, S.C.

Then things got ugly. The messengers wanted to get their names in and get back on the street earning again. A dozen or more in back of the room began to shove their way forward. Words were exchanged, and shouts turned to fists, a free-for-all in the making. Fortunately, the security staff moved in immediately and cleared the room.

Kathleen was left sitting in an empty room with nothing to show for the day but a very large hotel bill. The law firm never did hire its own messenger and still uses pay-by-the-piece outsiders.

*Advertising an open house is likely to draw a crowd
in a large metropolitan area. Consider asking for applications
by mail and pre-screening by telephone.*

# Mexican Revolt

*He who has money has in his pocket those who have none.*

Leo Tolstoy

The only word I could use to describe the owner of the small New Jersey company I worked for as chief financial officer was *cheap*. *Miser* fit, too. He could be charming and friendly, but *never* when money was involved.

I was looking for a controller at the time, and the ridiculously low salary he let me offer, combined with our location in a bad section of a large city, was severely hampering my search.

On Christmas Eve, though, the owner astonished me and everyone else. He ordered in mounds of food from a local delicatessen and threw a lunchtime party for the factory workers. When lunch was over, he climbed up on a table, shouted for quiet and announced, "We won't get much work done this afternoon, so we might as well close early and all go home."

The foreman translated his words for the factory workers, most of whom spoke only Spanish, and cheers broke out. Muchas gracias, señor. Gracias. Feliz Navidad! Feliz Navidad!

The next week I was lucky enough to get a good résumé from a woman applying for the controller's job. I had her come in, and she seemed perfect. I half expected her to walk out the door when we got to the part about salary, but she said she'd accept it if there was room for advancement.

I was about to offer her the job when loud shouting erupted from the owner's office next door. I excused myself to find out what was going on. An angry crowd of factory workers spilled out of his office into the hallway, all screaming in Spanish, waving their pay checks and shaking their fists. The foreman was nowhere to be seen.

It took me a few minutes to calm everybody down and discover the problem. It turned out that the owner had docked everyone a half-day's pay for Christmas Eve.

"But you told everyone to go home," I said to him.

"Sure, I did," he replied, "but I never said I was going to pay anyone for it. Now get these people out of here."

Eventually, the fuss died down and the workers straggled back into the plant. I went back to my office to continue the interview.

"What was going on?" she asked.

I was too embarrassed to tell her the truth, so I lied. "Oh, it was just a production meeting. Everybody is real excited about our new product line."

"Really?" she asked. "Then why were they shouting 'blood sucking parasite'?"

"I might as well tell you," she said, standing up. "I speak fluent Spanish, and this is not the kind of company I want to work for. Thank you for seeing me." With that she shook my hand and left.

Factory production that January was the lowest it had ever been, and I finally hired a controller at $5,000 a year more than I had offered the woman. The owner never did figure out that sometimes "cheap" turns out to be expensive.

*Sometimes it's time to say "no."*

# Pay Phone

*A good scare is worth more to a man than good advice.*
E.W. Howe

*Financial printers routinely handle extremely confidential and valuable corporate information, the kind that led to Wall Street's "insider trading" scandals a few years ago.*

I was personnel manager for a financial printer, and sorry that my phone number was in the ad for a pressman. The calls kept coming. "Hello. I'm calling about your ad for a pressman. My name is Marty."

I went through my list of qualifying technical questions and he answered them all, right on the button. Here was one I could be interested in.

"Marty, I'd like to see you. Can you come in tomorrow?"

"I'd love to," he replied, "but I don't get out of prison until Tuesday."

What is this, a joke? "Okay, Marty, call me when you get out."

Realizing that he was being put off, he pleaded, "No, wait, wait. I know how this must sound, but it's true, I'm really in prison. This is where I learned the trade, and I am a good pressman."

"Well, I'd like to help you, Marty, but we handle a lot of confidential material here. I don't think you'd be my best choice."

"I know what financial printing is," he said, "and believe me, I know that if any confidential information ever leaked out I'd be the prime suspect. That's why I'll be the most honest employee you ever had. I know what it's like in this place. I don't ever want to come back."

He was convincing, and I decided to take a chance. I brought Marty in as soon as he was free and had our pressroom foreman check out his skills. Marty was one of the best he'd ever seen, the foreman told me.

I hired Marty. It was one of the best decisions I ever made. When the pressroom foreman retired five years later, Marty got the job.

*Be honest about obvious negatives, and put the best interpretation on them you can. The person who is impressed by your candor and directness may give you a chance to prove yourself.*

**75**

# Full Size

*She looked as if she had been poured into*
*her clothes, and forgotten to say "when."*

P.G. Wodehouse

**P**aul's secretary had just quit without notice (her husband was transferred overseas) and the strategic plan was due — all 287 pages of text, charts, tables and graphs. It couldn't just *look* professional, it had to *be* professional, and Paul didn't know Aldus, Quark and PageMaker from Groucho, Harpo and Zeppo. He had to replace her immediately — Red Alert, Priority 1.

Dammit, he thought, what do I do now?

An "Urgent" ad in the paper drew 46 résumés in the first three days. He winnowed those down to ten possibles and said aloud, "Okay, ear, it's telephone time, prepare yourself."

Abigail sounded best. She understood the job (she'd produced budgets and business plans on deadline before; *she* described to Paul what it took, not vice versa), knew the software, and didn't mind overtime. She was also easy to talk to. Paul invited her in.

Abigail arrived…and was huge, 350 pounds at least.

"How do you do?" she said in her pleasing voice, "it's nice to meet you in person." Paul stared, stunned, but finally took the hand she offered and stammered, "Yah, uhh, well, uhh, thanks for coming in on short notice. Uhh, please, please come in, come in, have a seat," and gestured at his visitor's chair. It was straight-backed and had arms.

And Abigail didn't fit. She tried, but couldn't quite make it, finally perching on the edge, only half sitting. It must have been very uncomfortable, but she smiled and ignored it. Paul ran through the interview quickly. Then, "Abigail, thank you for coming in. I'll get back to you soon, one way or another."

She didn't move. At first Paul was afraid she was stuck. But she looked directly at him and said simply, "It's my weight isn't it? You're uncomfortable dealing with me because of my weight."

Flustered, Paul thought about it a moment, a dead giveaway and he realized it. Finally he answered, "To tell you the truth, Abigail, I need a certain chemistry with someone I work with. It's unfair, maybe, but I am uncomfortable around you."

She said nothing, just pulled a newspaper clipping from her purse and handed it to him, page B-12 of *The Wall Street Journal*, November 23, 1993. A woman had sued and won a $100,000 judgment. She'd been denied a job because she was obese. The Federal Appeals Court in Boston upheld the decision.

"Are you saying you're going to sue if you don't get the job?"

"I'm saying I'd like you to give me a chance. You liked my résumé. We got along wonderfully on the phone. I know I can do a good job for you. Let me prove it."

Decision time, thought Paul, as their eyes locked. What'll it be, reason or emotion? What she says is true. What I feel is real. Who's right?

"All right, Abigail, I'll give you a chance."

"Thank you, you won't be disappointed."

Within weeks, Paul knew that Abigail was the best secretary he'd ever had.

*Be direct, confident and positive.*

# Leisure Lunch

*Hard work never killed anybody,*
*but why take a chance?*

Edgar Bergen

oy landed the computer consulting spot at a national news magazine after several interviews, and was now in his first week on the job.

Every day at lunch time, out came his newspaper, and, feet up on the desk in his cubicle, he read it through. At 1 o'clock, he folded the paper away and got back to work.

The employees complained. "The guy's reading a *newspaper* at his desk, for God's sake!" the manager complained to the consulting firm that had placed Roy.

The sales rep from the consulting firm went to the magazine personally. "You're blowin' it, Roy. He doesn't like people reading newspapers in the office. Says it looks like his people are goofin' off. And he's the boss."

Roy was adamant. "It's my goddamn lunch hour, *my* time. If I want to read the paper on my time, I will. It's none of his goddamn business!"

Two days later Roy was terminated, and to this day feels he was unjustly wronged.

◎

*Observe the corporate culture, especially during a probationary period.*
*Right or wrong, justified or not, some behavior is considered*
*unacceptable and can shorten your tenure on a job.*

# Phone Interview

*That's an amazing invention,*
*but who would ever want to use one of them?*

President Rutherford B. Hayes
on seeing a demonstration of a telephone in 1876

**B**urt, chief financial officer of American Healthcare Manufacturing, a small New Jersey manufacturer of medical devices, needed a controller, and his ad in the *Star-Ledger* drew a huge response. Selecting two dozen "possibles," he set out to do some screening by telephone.

Damn, he thought, after two no-answers and four answering machines, they're all home numbers and nobody's home. He resigned himself to staying late and making his calls that evening.

After a dull cafeteria dinner and a few chapters in a mystery novel, 8 o'clock rolled around and he picked up the phone to call the first name on his list.

"Hello?"

"Hello," said Burt briskly. "Is this David Clayton?"

"Yes?"

"Mr. Clayton, my name is Burt McGarry from American Healthcare..."

"Sorry, I don't need any insurance." Click!

Burt blinked at the phone. Insurance? He dialed Clayton's number again.

"Hello?"

"Hello, Mr. Clayton," Burt said quickly, "please don't hang up — you sent us your résumé!"

"Oh. Oh! Oh, I'm sorry."

"That's okay, I understand."

But every call went that way, despite the fact that Burt had included his company's name in the ad, as well as a description of their products and target market.

By 9 pm he'd had enough of phones slamming in his ear and then doing the call-back routine. He was beginning to feel real compassion for all the telemarketing people who'd called him over the years.

Okay, one more, he thought, and I'll pick the best of the bunch. He pulled out Fred Johnson's résumé, the one to beat in his mind from the

**79**

beginning, and steeling himself for another bout of misunderstanding, dialed the Johnson residence.

A woman's voice answered. "Yes?"

"Is this Mrs. Johnson?" Burt asked.

"Yes."

"May I please speak to your husband?"

"Who's calling?"

"My name is Burt McGarry, from American Healthcare Manufacturing, and he..."

"Just a minute." She put the phone down before Burt could finish. He heard her call out, "There's some guy on the phone from Health-care something or other, asking for you."

A male voice in the background answered, faint but clear, "Tell him I'm not home. I don't need any health care tonight."

Burt frowned. Then he heard the phone being picked up, and Mrs. Johnson again. "I'm sorry," she said, "he isn't home right now."

Yeah, sure, thought Burt. Well, the hell with it. "All right," he said to Mrs. Johnson. "When he gets in please have him call me. He sent me his résumé for our controller's position."

"He did? I, uh...oh, wait! Wait! I think I hear his car pulling into the garage." She put down the phone again. This time Burt could barely hear her whisper, "This guy is calling about a job! I told him you just got home. Quick! Pick up the phone."

Footsteps approached, and this time a male voice spoke into Burt's ear. "Fred Johnson here," he said, "glad I got in when I did! Bad traffic tonight, ha ha."

Burt scowled at the phone. "Is that right?" he asked sarcastically. "Well, let me tell you something, Fred Johnson, my friend. First, I'm staying late in the office tonight to make these calls, and you've just wasted a considerable chunk of my time playing hide-and-seek with me."

"But I thought..."

"Second," Burt went on, "you and your wife both lied to me."

"But she..."

"And third, you showed me that you're conducting such an unprofessional job search that you can't even remember who you sent your résumé to!"

"But..."

"So you'll excuse me for having some reservations about your overall organizational and professional abilities!"

"I..."

"I have a stack of two dozen résumés here," said Burt, "and believe me when I tell you, it won't take much to drop yours in the wastebasket!"

He hung up and, with considerable satisfaction, filed Fred Johnson's résumé in the trash.

◎

*When you send out your résumé, know where you sent it*
*and be prepared to answer calls at any time. Consider keeping*
*a list by your telephone of companies you contacted.*

# Honest Man

*After all, when you have to kill a man it costs nothing to be polite.*
Winston Churchill

Originally from Denmark and now a marketing executive for an insurance company in Los Angeles, Hannah had two staff positions to fill — ASAP. In addition to advertising the openings, she asked her employees to recommend qualified people.

"Good, set up an interview," she replied immediately when a product manager said her cousin John was available and knew the field.

John came in and was impressive — well dressed and over six feet tall with shoulders filling the doorway. Hannah admired the image for a moment, then said, "Close the door, John, so we can have some privacy. Let's sit over here on the couch to talk." She never liked interviewing people with a desk between them.

After some easy small talk, John leaned forward, suddenly intense, and spoke: *"I want you to know that I've killed two people."*

Hannah's jaw dropped. Her eyes darted instinctively to the closed solid oak door, but his massive frame blocked the way. The phone was on the other side of the desk.

John leaned further forward, reaching into his briefcase, and Hannah instinctively recoiled. He handed her his résumé. It said he'd just gotten out of prison after serving ten years for manslaughter, and listed his parole officer's name where most résumés list references.

After the bombshell, Hannah stayed nervous but John became charming and easy going again. She wondered what prompted a man who seemed so like any other professional to take the lives of two people. In any case, she was relieved when the interview ended.

Hannah didn't hire John, but insists it was because he lacked experience — ten years missing from his career. She says she believes in giving people a second chance and would have interviewed him even if she'd known about his prison record.

*Ex-offenders should consider career development workshops offered,
often free, by some state employment centers, parole bureaus
and community-based organizations such as
The Fortune Society in New York City.*

# The Gap

*Men have called me mad; but the question is not yet settled,*
*whether madness is or is not the loftiest intelligence.*

Edgar Allan Poe

aren pushed open the door to Jocko Sullivan's, her favorite cafe, and went straight to the bar. She took a seat, ordered a scotch and downed it in a gulp.

Mel, the bartender, raised an eyebrow.

"Don't start, Mel," she said, raising a hand. "Just pour another one of those bad boys."

The other eyebrow went up.

"No, no, I promise to nurse this one," Karen said, smiling. She pushed back an errant strand of hair.

"It has been, I take it, a day?" asked Mel, refilling her glass.

"It has been that," she said, nodding. "Ah, thanks. Mud in your eye."

"To you, too," said Mel. "So what's the story?"

"Okay." Karen settled herself on the stool. "You know I'm a recruiter, right?"

Mel nodded. "I've heard you speak about it. Wall Street, right?"

"Exactly. So, this week I'm trying to fill a back-office position."

"You lost me. What's a back-office position?" Mel asked.

"For a brokerage firm," she said. "It's off-site space, in this case over in Jersey City, where the clerks and number crunchers do their thing. No sense paying rent downtown here where space is so expensive, so a lot of firms park their support people and computers in some back-office somewhere."

"I get it," said Mel.

She nodded. "Anyway, this one guy I saw today had a résumé with about 20 years' experience in the back-office. Perfect, you'd think, right?"

"I would."

"Well, wait. He comes in, and he's the meekest little guy you'd ever want to see. A real Casper Milquetoast. Big mild eyes, wispy gray hair, a complete mouse.

"Not that that matters if you're working in a back-office, though. All the flashy types in sales and trading work down here on Wall Street. So who cares what the techies look like in Jersey City."

"That makes sense," said Mel, drawing off a draft for one of the cocktail waitresses.

"Anyway, I didn't give it a lot of thought, because the interview went well. He had all the qualifications and experience I was looking for. Then I asked him about this gap in his résumé."

"Gap?" Mel asked.

Karen nodded. "Yeah, nine months unaccounted for since he left his last job. Back-office work doesn't pay that kind of severance, so I asked him about it. You won't believe what he told me."

"Try me. I'm a bartender, remember?"

"He told me flat out that he'd spent the last nine months in a state hospital! After trying to kill his wife! With an ax!"

"Really? Come on! And you believed him?"

"Yeah, Mel, I did. If anybody else told me that, I'd laugh. But there was something about this guy — a constant monotone, no inflection at all

in his voice. His eyes were kind of flat and lifeless. Absolutely zero emotion in his face. Yeah, Mel, I believed him. I figure he was still on some kind of drug to keep him calm."

"So what'd you do?"

"Well, right away I said I had another appointment, excused myself and went and got this big young guy we have in the office. He finished up for me."

Mel picked up the scotch bottle and filled two glasses.

"This one's on the house," he said, pushing one toward her and raising his own glass. "Here's to tomorrow!"

Karen is now a personal trainer, but swears she didn't leave recruiting because of "the ax man."

*Job-search counseling for people with physical, mental and socially disabling conditions such as alcoholism is available through vocational rehabilitation programs sponsored by the Federal Government's Rehabilitation Services Administration and State Departments of Labor or Education.*

# Verbal Volcano

*Hating people is like burning down your own house to kill a rat.*

Harry Emerson Fosdick

Tony, a management consulting associate, jumped at the big pharmaceutical company's job search assignment for a highly specialized contract employee. *Two* people in his database met the obscure requirements. He arranged interviews for both and sent the strongest first.

The first candidate reported back that "I'm not sure the interviewer knows what she wants, but her accent was so heavy I couldn't tell what she was saying anyway."

But during the debriefing, he suddenly lit up. "Ahhh, *that's* what she was driving at! Now I see it." And he explained to Tony the interviewer's line of questioning that he hadn't understood earlier — with all the proper answers.

Tony passed this information along to the second candidate, William, who made good use of it. Even though he was only marginally qualified, *he* got the job.

It took just three months for the pharmaceutical company to realize that William was not technically up to the job and had serious interpersonal problems as well. On a Friday afternoon, the company informed Tony of their intention to terminate William for unsatisfactory performance.

The following Monday, Tony visited the company and William's manager explained the situation. She said she'd give two weeks' notice. Tony told William...who exploded like a verbal volcano — ranting, screaming, cursing.

"Cool it," Tony warned him. "They're letting you stay for two weeks. Keep this up and you could lose that, too." William calmed down and Tony drove back to his office almost an hour away.

When he arrived, the pharmaceutical manager was on the phone. "William's out of control," she told him. "He's obnoxious, raging around, abusing and intimidating people. Get him out of here today! We'll give you a week's pay for him, but get him out of here now!"

Tony turned around and drove back to the company. "You blew it," he told William. "You cost yourself a week's pay and they want you out of the building now. Let's go." William continued his rampage but let Tony lead him out.

He followed Tony back to the management consultant's office, barged in and demanded the full two weeks' pay. No, the president told him. One week is all we're getting, that's all you'll get.

"Then stuff it!" William raged, storming out the door. Minutes later, he returned and agreed to the one week's pay.

Days later, he appeared in the pharmaceutical company's parking lot to demand the extra week's pay from the manager who terminated him, threatening other employees as well. When he showed up a second time, the company called the police but he was gone before they arrived.

Then William wrote to the pharmaceutical company's president demanding the two weeks' pay and threatening a demonstration at the plant, using Al Sharpton to organize and publicize his plight as racial prejudice if they refused. The company put in another call to Tony. They all agreed to ignore the letter.

It was several weeks after that when Tony stopped to buy gasoline, and suddenly there was William outside his car window, wild eyed and demanding that *Tony* pay him the second week's wages. Screaming "Get outta the car, get outta the car," he threatened to beat Tony up if he didn't pay it.

Tony locked the doors and leaned on his horn, attracting a police patrol car. William immediately launched into an elaborate story of how "this fat honky" was discriminating against him and cheating him out of a week's pay.

The policeman made it plain to William: if I see you in this town again, you'll be arrested.

The officer followed Tony back to the office for corroboration, and the management consulting company got a restraining order the next day. William hasn't been seen since.

*Pre-screening candidates is a critical component of the consulting firm's obligation to the client company. Failure to pre-screen adequately can be a reputation wrecker for the consulting company (and the candidate).*

# Shave and a Haircut

*Nothing so needs reforming as other people's habits.*

Mark Twain

**B**efore his interview at a major Wall Street investment bank, the programmer/analyst, as instructed, walked into the consulting company's office — long hair unwashed and in rat-tails, two-day beard, flannel shirt and jeans, smelling like he'd slept with a pig.

"Do you know where you're going, what kind of firm this is?" the recruiter asked.

"Sure," the candidate answered casually. "Look, I overslept. I didn't have time to shower."

"You've got plenty of time now, pal! Because there's no way you're going on the interview!"

*Get a good night's sleep before the interview*
*and get up early enough to shower and dress appropriately.*

# Fast Track

*Be yourself is the worst advice to give some people.*

Tom Masson

*"Open house" is a proven method of screening many job candidates in a short time. It's a grueling, exhausting day, but an effective recruiting tool. I was interviewing for sales people at an open house outside Washington, D.C.*

t 8:55, I peeked out the meeting room door and reported back: "Fifty or sixty at least milling around out there." The others groaned.

"Nine o'clock," called a woman from her table along the wall. "Let's herd 'em in."

The first person through the door — a tall, thin young man in a pin-striped suit, very professional — headed straight for me.

"I'm Josh Whitley," he said, shaking my hand with a firm grip and exuding the confidence every good sales rep needs. He sat down, glancing at his watch, and we started to talk.

As I described the company, our product lines and customers, he glanced down at his watch every two or three minutes.

"You keep checking the time. Do you have another appointment?"

"Oh no, no," he replied easily.

Nevertheless, he kept peeking at his watch as we talked, to the point where, exasperated, I insisted: "Josh, something's wrong. You have a problem with the time. What is it?"

"Well, the track opens at 11," he said. "I don't want to be late. Is this going to take much longer?"

With a smile, I stood and extended my hand. "No, Josh, we just finished. Good luck at the track."

*Keep all your attention on the interview to show
that you really want the job.*

*If the job holds little interest for the candidate,
it's clearly a mismatch and an easy "no" for the interviewer.*

# Refreshments

*Semper Fidelis*
*(Always Faithful)*
U.S. Marine Corps motto

Cathy was interviewing for an executive position at Pizza Hut, a division of PepsiCo (manufacturer of Pepsi Cola), and she was on a roll until....

"Want some coffee, Cathy?" the interviewer asked.

"Thanks, but I'd rather have a Coke."

The interview was effectively over; the job and Cathy were gone.

# Overnight Delivery

*His messengers ride forth East and West and South and North.*
Thomas Babington,
"Lays of Ancient Rome," 1842

Donna was excited about the job she saw advertised at Purolator Courier, an overnight delivery company, and wanted her résumé to be among the first to get there. She sent it by Federal Express...and was immediately eliminated from consideration.

*Remember where you're interviewing.*
*Brand loyalty is a job requirement.*

Chapter 4

# Unexpected Circumstances

# Power Lunch

*Bulls can make money and Bears can make money —
but Pigs always lose.*

Wall Street saying

lbert kicked open the door of his Columbia University dorm room, flung his arms wide and announced, "I've got the job!"

Max, his roommate, looked up from a physics text. "Uh-huh. And what makes you so certain, my bourgeois friend?"

"Remember last week when I interviewed on campus for that financial associate's spot?"

Max nodded. "The Wall Street investment bank," he said.

"Indeed," said Albert. "And you, in your typically callow manner, opined that it was a waste of my time and theirs."

"I did, didn't I," said Max with satisfaction.

"Well, you were wrong!" Albert said triumphantly. "I just got a call from said Wall Street bank — said *blue chip* Wall Street bank, peasant — from Mr. Harvey Coudert, the very man who interviewed me. And we're going to lunch on Friday. A posh downtown beanery called..." consulting the note in his hand, "Fraunces Tavern."

"Well, well," said Max. "Never heard of it."

Albert dropped into an old overstuffed chair. "Me either," he confided. "But I bet our friend Jeffrey Acheson the Bloody Third has. And he's just the lad I intend to speak with before this lunch."

"A wise decision," said Max dryly. "Your idea of haute cuisine leans towards MacDonald's. You shouldn't venture into any eatery above the Bowery without a little foreknowledge."

"Spoken like the true homeless person you are destined to become."

Later that day Albert visited Jeffrey Acheson, scion of a wealthy family from Westport, Connecticut. Despite his airy manner, Albert was sensitive about his lower-middle class background. "I'm more worried about the meal than I am about the interview," he admitted, explaining his plight to Jeffrey.

"No need," said Jeffrey, smiling reassuringly. "The first thing you have to do is relax. This Coudert guy already thinks you're a hot prospect, or he wouldn't have invited you out to lunch. Now, Fraunces Tavern is one

**92**

of the oldest restaurants in New York City. It's where George Washington gave a farewell dinner for his officers after the Revolution. Everybody who's anybody on Wall Street...well, you finish that sentence."

Albert stirred nervously. "I was sort of hoping that a place with 'tavern' in its name means I could just get a quick sandwich and a beer."

Jeffrey shook his head, grinning. "Not this one, Albert."

"Well, then, what do I order?"

"Not a problem," said Jeffrey. "Seriously. Order the London broil, medium rare."

"Is that like chuck steak or something?"

"Close enough," said Jeffrey. "You'll love it. For God's sake, though, don't order it well done."

"Huh? Why not? I like my meat well done."

"Well, that's a good cut we're talking about, and only a Philistine would want it cooked that way."

Albert frowned. "Oh."

Jeffrey nodded. "For a drink, suggest a bottle of Mouton Cadet Red. Don't get white wine with the London broil."

"I don't usually drink at lunch," said Albert, "but if you say so. What about the cost?"

"The bank will pick up the tab, you can forget that," Jeffrey answered. "As far as the wine, you're invited to a 'power lunch' here. You can't wimp out and order beer."

On Friday, Albert was nervous despite Jeffrey's coaching. He took a cab from Columbia down to the tip of Manhattan. The ride cost him $25, but it was better than arriving hot and sweaty from the subway.

The restaurant, though decidedly upscale, was not as posh as Albert had feared. Mr. Coudert was waiting for him in the bar. "Right on time, Albert," he said, extending his hand. "Glad you could make it." He seemed friendly, and Albert began to feel better.

He ordered lunch exactly as Jeffrey had suggested: London broil medium rare and a bottle of Mouton Cadet Red. He felt assured when the waiter said, "Very good, sir," with a warm smile.

But Albert was uneasy again when the waiter took Mr. Coudert's order. "Just the diet salad and Perrier," he said.

Albert managed to carry off tasting a sip of the wine when it came, nodding sagely to the waiter and ignoring the proffered cork. Jeffrey had said that cork-smelling was considered declassé by those truly in the know.

The London broil really was good, but he felt a bit guilty eating it while Mr. Coudert munched away on a salad. The wine was definitely a mistake, he decided. Mr. Coudert politely declined any. "Have to work this afternoon, you know," he said.

Albert didn't want to appear as if he were wasting good wine, so he felt obliged to drink it. After half the bottle, though, he gave up. He was beginning to feel tipsy.

They spoke about sports during lunch. It was not until coffee (they both declined dessert) that Mr. Coudert finally got around to business.

"Albert, I wanted to speak with you today personally, not as a representative of the bank. Unfortunately, you see, we've decided to fill the associate's position with an individual who interned with us last summer. You'll be getting a formal letter in a few days."

Albert's heart sank. No job. And he could just hear Max's comments. He debated pouring another glass of wine.

"However," Mr. Coudert went on cheerfully, "I wanted to tell you how very impressed I was with your qualifications. If you give me a few extra copies of your résumé, I'll be happy to pass them along to some friends of mine. I just wanted to have lunch with you to say good luck and don't get discouraged."

A waiter came and handed the check to Mr. Coudert, who looked at it for what seemed an eternity. Albert's heart sank further with a sudden, horrible suspicion. Mr. Coudert had stressed he was not acting as a representative of the bank. Could that mean...?

Mr. Coudert looked up from the check and said, "Albert, usually I'd just split this down the middle, but after all, I only had a small salad. Your portion comes to $43.75."

After the taxi ride, Albert had only $12 cash in his pocket. He didn't own a credit card and didn't have a check with him.

"Um, look, Mr. Coudert, uh, this is awfully embarrassing. Um, you see, I've only got $12 on me. Can you possibly lend me the money to pay for this? I'll put a check in the mail this afternoon."

Mr. Coudert gave Albert a wintry smile. "I see. Well, okay, Albert," he said coolly, "I guess that's not a problem." He paid the waiter and accepted Albert's $12.

And somehow he managed to leave the restaurant without taking any copies of Albert's résumé, but not before writing down his office address where Albert could send him a check for $31.75.

Feeling dismal, Albert followed him out of the restaurant. As he stood on the sidewalk, disconsolately watching Mr. Coudert walk away through the lunchtime crowd, another horrible thought struck him.

I don't have any money to get back to campus! He was, he knew, about as far from Columbia as he could get on Manhattan Island. In a moment of panic, he actually considered running after Mr. Coudert to borrow money for the subway, but the moment passed.

Finally, emboldened by the wine, he took his only other option. He went down into the subway and jumped the turnstile, the first time he'd ever done it. A loud "Hey!" came from the clerk in the token booth, and he ran for the platform. A train was just pulling in, and he ducked inside, picturing himself being dragged off to jail in handcuffs. Luckily, there were no Transit Police at the station, and the train pulled out.

After switching to the wrong trains twice, Albert finally made it back to Columbia. When he got to his room, he was relieved to find that Max wasn't there. He emptied his pockets on the desk, hung up his suit and took a shower.

Afterward, he picked up the paper with Mr. Coudert's address on it.

"You know something, Mr. Coudert?" he said to the paper. "I figure that between the aggravation of schlepping down to that restaurant in the first place when you could have told me on the phone, plus all the preparation I did, plus risking getting busted for fare-jumping, and getting lost twice in the bowels of the earth, you and I are pretty much square!"

Slowly and carefully, he tore up the paper in little pieces and tossed them in the trash.

*It's common practice to invite a candidate for lunch or dinner to observe the "real person" in an informal, non-business environment. Be warned—it's part of the evaluation process.*

# Researcher

*Ninety-nine percent of all surprises in business are negative.*

Harold Geneen
CEO, ITT, 1984

**W**hat's the problem? Good résumé. Lots of interviews. *No call-backs!* John was doing something wrong.

He sat down to evaluate himself. Okay, man, the truth! Intelligence? Above average. Education and grades? Good. Work experience? Light, but good companies. Personality? Hell, I was born and raised in Texas, a storyteller, get along with all the interviewers, no problem there. Preparation? Yeah...preparation! That must be it. I "wing it" at every interview, know nothing about the company except what I pick up in the lobby. Well, I can fix that!

A few days later, a recruiter called. "John, got an interview for you."

"What? I can't hear you. Who's this?"

"John, it's me, Sarah, I'm on the car phone. Look, you have an interview with American Standard...." The connection was so bad he had her repeat the address twice.

Okay, man, this time prepare! He looked up everything he could find about American Standard, a large manufacturer of kitchen and bath fixtures — used *Moody's, Standard & Poor's* and *Value Line* reports, searched *The Wall Street Journal* and Dow Jones articles for the past year, checked brokerage research reports — and memorized it all, even the names of their Board of Directors.

He set out for that interview more prepared than he'd ever been...and realized his mistake when he got there. It wasn't American Standard, the toilet company, it was Standard Brands, the food company. John was completely unprepared.

And totally shaken. He couldn't even think of a joke or a funny story to tell. John just sat there, kept his mouth shut and listened. A couple of times, he pointed out his specific experience. He was too embarrassed to admit that he'd researched the wrong firm.

He got the job and moved into senior management.

*Cultivate your listening skills. Talking too much
in an interview can be as bad as not saying enough.*

# More Fun Than . . .

*People will soon get tired of staring at a plywood box every night.*

Darryl Zanuck
Head of 20th Century Fox,
commenting on television in 1946

Elsie Farrell, my mother, was an actress. She'd done a few bit parts and minor TV commercials, but always dreamed of making it big in The Big Time—New York City.

In the early 1960s, we lived in Connecticut and Elsie was doing a series of very low budget commercials out of New Haven's local Channel 8 for W.T. Grant, a discount department store.

"One-Take Elsie," the crew called her. With her stage training, she could read over the script, deliver it flawlessly and wrap up shooting before lunch. She hoped to ride her high quality, low cost reputation all the way to the big city.

Her break came when a producer of commercials from New York was planning to visit his son at Yale anyway, and agreed to stop by Channel 8 to watch Elsie shoot one of her commercials.

The day came. The New York producer arrived. And Elsie got the script ten minutes before shooting, as usual. The commercial was for a big plastic dump truck, with a child playing with it on camera while Elsie did the scripted voice-over: "rugged...inexpensive...fun...more fun than a barrel of monkeys" (even then, advertising writers loved clichés).

"Ready, people?" the director called. "Okay...action!"

The child played with the truck as two cameras rolled and Elsie's most persuasive voice flowed onto the tape with perfect diction and tone: "rugged...inexpensive...fun...more fun than a barrel of *money.*"

Laughter filled the studio, and a muscular old cameraman with U.S. Navy tattooed on his forearm called, "Attagirl, Elsie, there ain't nothin' more fun than a barrel of money!" Even the New York producer laughed.

"Okay, people, okay," the director called, "calm down now and get serious. Let's do it again. Ready?"

If the second take had gone well, the flub would have been funny and forgotten. But Elsie was flustered. Her one-take record was shattered, and she was blowing her big chance. Again she said the line, "...more fun than a barrel of money." There were just a few chuckles this time.

By the tenth take, she still couldn't get it straight and the humor was

**98**

all gone. Overtime and over-budget threatened. There was even talk of calling the sponsor to change the script, but Elsie vetoed that. She at least wanted to prove she could do it correctly if not quickly.

The New York producer was a gentleman throughout, and stayed for the entire fiasco. Finally, on take twelve, Elsie got out "...more fun than a barrel of monkeys" with perfect enthusiasm, and the director called it a wrap.

The closest Elsie ever came to The Big Time in New York was as an extra on *Car 54, Where Are You?*

The only one happy that day in New Haven was the little boy who got to play with the truck through all twelve takes — me. I even got to keep the truck. Looking back on it now, Elsie was probably right the first time. To a child, a toy *is* more fun than a barrel of money.

*"If you aim your dreams high and fall short,*
*you can still land high."*
Rev. Stevan J. Thayer, Interfaith Minister

**99**

# Barcelona Games

*You can't make a dime on the Olympics.*

Unnamed New York City bookie

I t was Madrid, 1991, a year before the XXV Summer Olympiad in Barcelona. Miguel had helped his firm win the $15 million technical systems design project to support the games and disseminate on-line information to the world. Now he needed a top-notch computer person to manage the 150 techies working on it. Carlos, a freelance consultant from Barcelona, came highly recommended.

Miguel barely started the interview when he was called away to a crisis meeting. "I'll wait," Carlos assured him. But when Miguel finally returned over five hours later, Carlos had headed home and Miguel didn't blame him. That takes guts, he thought, the kind whoever gets this job will need. I want him!

So Miguel caught a plane for Barcelona, too. He arrived at Carlos's door with an apology, wine, flowers and a gift for his wife, and took them to dinner at the city's finest restaurant. Carlos, it turned out, was indeed his man. When he asked for $50,000 Miguel offered $70,000. The deal was closed, a good deal for everybody.

Carlos flawlessly managed the systems' development and day-to-day operation during the games — a talented, effective senior consultant! He was so good, in fact, that when a large American company approached Miguel about Carlos after the games, Miguel lied and said he was paying $110,000. The company hired Carlos for $150,000.

*When a talented interviewer recognizes a talented candidate,*
*it is worthwhile to pursue the candidate.*

# Quite a Background

*Let me have no lying; it becomes none but tradesmen.*

William Shakespeare, *The Winter's Tale*

The recruiter received Gil's résumé with nothing but praise for his computer training and experience. "Quite a background you have for such a young man. Just one thing. The résumé looks a little sloppy. I'll have someone here redo it for you. Saves time. I have three or four places I'd like to submit it right away."

And sure enough, two days later Gil got a call to talk with a large company in Indianapolis that had his résumé from the recruiter.

He met with the management information systems (MIS) director, and the interview went well. At first. Then came some very technical questions about Honeywell computers.

"I don't know much about Honeywells," Gil answered honestly, "but I've done a lot of work on IBMs."

"But it says right here you have 'extensive experience on Honeywell computers,'" the director noted, pointing to Gil's résumé.

"There must be some mix-up," Gil replied. "May I look at that?"

His name and address were correct, but the background was totally different. Either the recruiter had put his name on someone else's résumé by mistake, or he'd deliberately changed it to fit the job requirements.

Gil explained the situation and apologized profusely. He also went over his true background, and later sent the MIS director a thank-you note with a copy of his real résumé (retyped).

He didn't get that job, but he'd impressed the director. A few weeks later, when an IBM operator's job opened up, the company offered it to Gil. He took it happily, and the recruiter got no fee.

Gil later moved successfully into computer sales, and today owns his own retail computer store in Somerville, New Jersey.

*If you find yourself fielding a recruiter's foul ball, it's an opportunity to look good. It's easy to say "This is what I do." Follow up with a résumé and letter expressing your interest in joining the firm.*

# Sign Here

*I would sooner be esteemed an ignoramus than a liar.*

Benedetto Varchi (1502-1565)

M r. Lloyd, the recruiting manager, had good news. "Well, Mitch," he said, "I think we have a place for you in our experimental engine group. You're shy on experience, but your educational background is good. If you'd like to join us, you can start on Monday." Mitch accepted enthusiastically.

Two weeks later, he was deep in a fluid dynamics problem on his CAD workstation when the Security Office called him in. Mitch assumed it was to pick up his employee ID card.

But he was ushered into a stark conference room with three large men he had never seen before, all dressed in identical gray suits. When he saw the tape recorder on the table, he was puzzled, a little uneasy.

The man at the head of the table had iron-gray hair cropped short and prominent jowls. He stood up without offering to shake hands. "Good morning Mister, ah, Russell. I am John Dexter, vice president of security." He didn't introduce the other two. "As you may have noticed, this conversation is being recorded. Do you have any objection?"

Mitch blinked. He looked at the other men, and they looked back at him. "Uh..." His voice broke. "Uh, no sir, no, that's okay. What's this all about?"

"Good," said Dexter. "Sit down, Russell, please. Now, would you mind describing for us exactly how you came to work here?"

"Well, uh, sure," Mitch began. "I studied engineering in college, where I got real interested in ways to improve the burn efficiency of gasoline, and I wrote a paper on ..."

Dexter held up a large hand. "Not *that* far back, Russell. Just tell us how you applied for this job."

"Oh. Well, I saw an ad in the newspaper and I ..."

Again Dexter interrupted. "You didn't go through a recruiting firm called Excel Engineering Placement?"

"Who?" asked Mitch, blinking. "No. I didn't go through any recruiters. The ad said to send résumés directly to the Human Resources Department."

One of the other men at the table leaned over to his associate and whispered something Mitch couldn't hear.

"So you never had any dealings with Excel?" Dexter repeated.

"No, I already told you that."

The second man at the table slid a piece of paper over to Mitch. "Read that," he instructed, without bothering to introduce himself. It was an invoice to the company from Excel Engineering Placement in the amount of $10,000 for "services relating to the recruitment and placement of Mitchell Russell."

"I never heard of them," said Mitch.

The third man slid over another paper. It was a contract between Excel Engineering Placement and Mitchell Russell, giving Excel the exclusive right to represent him in any employment or salary negotiations.

"At the bottom," said the unidentified man. "Is that your signature?"

Mitch looked and swallowed hard. It was. Not a forgery or a photocopy, it was his signature in blue ballpoint.

Despite the air conditioning, he felt himself beginning to sweat. "That's my signature," he said, "and I know how this looks, but I never signed this."

"Well if you didn't, who did?" demanded the third man.

"I don't know how it got there," Mitch insisted, "but I never signed anything with Excel or any other placement agency."

"When you came in for an interview, you spoke to Mr. Lloyd in Human Resources. Is that correct?" Dexter asked.

"Yes," Mitch replied.

"We suspect Lloyd's been taking kickbacks from Excel," Dexter said, "and we're considering filing criminal charges against them both. We're here today to decide if we should also take action against you, Mr. Russell. You could be in a lot of trouble."

"But I never signed anything, I didn't do anything wrong," Mitch protested, knowing how lame that sounded. He was now sweating profusely. Every movie he'd ever seen about innocent men being convicted and sent to prison popped into his head.

"I want you to tell me every detail of the day you came here to interview," said Dexter. Over the next two hours, Mitch went over every minute of that day — starting with Mr. Lloyd, how he went on to talk with the heads of eight different engineering departments, took a tour through the engine design labs and wound up back in Mr. Lloyd's office.

"And that was it," Mitch said at last. His throat was dry, and he was tired of being grilled like a criminal. "At that point, I was exhausted, excited and late for my flight home, so I just signed the confidentiality agreement and...."

"Hold it," Dexter interrupted, "what confidentiality agreement?"

"Your standard form," said Mitch. "Mr. Lloyd told me everyone who tours the labs has to sign one. You're in security, you should know that."

"What did it look like? Did you *read* the form before you signed it, Mr. Russell?" Dexter asked slowly.

"Well, uh, no, not really," Mitch answered. "It was the end of the day, like I told you, and I was tired and in a hurry to catch my plane."

Dexter stood up and said, "Thank you for coming in, Mr. Russell. You can go back to work now."

Mitch was too scared to do anything but get up and leave.

A week later, Dexter called Mitch to say he was completely cleared. Lloyd had been doctoring the files of every engineer hired through newspaper ads to look as if they'd come through Excel, and then splitting the recruiting fees.

"Don't feel bad, Mitch," Dexter added. "You're not the only one who signed that paper, just the only one to tell us about it."

*You can find corruption in any industry. Read everything,*
*including the fine print, before you sign on the dotted line.*
*Only a hustler will fault you for it.*

# First Impression

*One writes a letter, taking particular trouble
to set it up as prettily as possible . . . .*

Sei Shonagon, b. 966

Just out of high school in Brooklyn, New York, Mary Ann was looking for her first job, and had no idea how to go about it.

She picked up a free "throwaway" newspaper in the grocery store, not the best place to look for career opportunities, and searched the ads. Cars for sale, automatic rug cleaners, hundreds of products and services. And of course the personals, whole pages filled with people of various types and tastes looking for romantic liaisons.

She was about to toss it when she spotted the tiny ad for a receptionist in a podiatrist's office a few blocks away. She wrote, outlining her qualifications, and two days later he called and offered her the job without even an interview. She started the next morning.

"I'm happy you hired me, doctor, I appreciate your confidence. But I'm curious. Why did you choose my letter out of all the others?"

The doctor laughed outright. "I'm sorry, Mary Ann, I'm not laughing at you. I've only been practicing a few weeks, and I didn't know anything about hiring people. I put an ad in that paper because it only cost $3. Look in the top desk drawer there, and you'll see all the other responses I got."

She opened the drawer and found two letters, both handwritten, one in pencil and the other — Mary Ann still swears to this — in crayon! She was crushed.

"You mean I got the job because you only got three responses and mine was the only one typed?"

"Yours was the only one I could read," the doctor chuckled, "and I had to have someone in here this morning."

Mary Ann eventually went on to better things. Today she's a school teacher, ironically, married to another podiatrist. On weekends, she sometimes fills in as his receptionist.

*It pays to have a professional-looking résumé.*

# Back East

*Go west young man.*

John Soule

It doesn't fit! Bill was horrified.

After five years in Los Angeles, he was back in New York for a career-jump job interview with a conservative, old-line brokerage house, and his old winter suit didn't fit! He sucked in his gut and struggled to close the three-inch gap between button and buttonhole and finally did, but he couldn't breathe much less sit down.

No good. It'll have to stay open. He hauled the zipper up as far as he could, put on his wide new belt to cover the gap and donned the jacket, which he didn't have to button. Not too bad, he appraised.

Confidence somewhat restored, Bill took a cab to the interview and met with the head of management information systems (MIS). When he offered a tour of the computer room, Bill accepted enthusiastically.

Leaving the office, the MIS director accidentally knocked some papers off the desk and Bill, without thinking, bent over to pick them up. *Riiiippppp!* The entire seam! His full backside gaped out at the world.

Bill straightened up slowly, back to the wall. "Um...uh...."

"Yes," the director sympathized, "you must be uncomfortable."

"You have no idea. Look, maybe I'd better just...."

"No, three people are waiting for you. Hold on, I'll be right back."

He returned with a long white lab coat. "Here, put this on."

For the rest of the day, Bill walked around meeting people and interviewing in the lab coat. He was sure he heard giggles behind him everywhere he went.

"Drop it off at the hotel's front desk when you check out," the MIS director told him. "I'll have somebody pick it up tomorrow."

The following day, Bill was back in Los Angeles wearing a loose summer suit that fit. He bought lunch in the park, a double-bacon-cheeseburger and a milkshake, and sat eating it in the warm sunshine. I don't think I want to live back East anyway, he thought contentedly.

*Try on your interview clothes before it's too late to replace them.*

# French, German & COBOL

*Q: How many programmers does it take to change a light bulb?*

*A: None. It's a hardware problem.*

**L**orie was an electrical engineer just out of the University of Delaware, graduating near the top of her class with an electrical engineering degree. During the first semester of her sophomore year there, she saw the movie *2001: A Space Odyssey* and she knew. Circuitry! She wanted to design digital circuits that could run anything — computers, telecommunications, space programs, the world!

She'd interviewed on campus with Bell Labs, Digital Equipment, DuPont, Hewlett-Packard, IBM and Raytheon, and to her delight, got a call from Bell Labs to come visit them on-site. And here she was. They had a full day of interviews scheduled with seven different departments, dinner that evening and a reservation for her at a nearby hotel.

"Hi, Lorie?" said a friendly voice only a few minutes after she'd signed in. It came from a smiling, well dressed man in his forties. "I'm Jerry Blodgett," he said as she stood up and shook hands.

Jerry led her to the cafeteria, bought coffee and they chatted.

"One thing, though, and I have to apologize," he said. "I haven't actually seen your résumé yet. All I have is the write-up and recommendation from your campus interview."

Lorie smiled, sipping the last of her coffee. "I hope he said something good. Here's another copy of my résumé."

"He did or you wouldn't be here," Jerry said, taking the résumé. "So tell me, what languages do you know?"

Lorie blinked. "Languages? Well, uh, I read and speak French and understand a little German..."

Jerry laughed. "No, seriously, what mainframe programming languages do you know?"

An alarm bell rang in her head. "I don't know any mainframe languages. I'm a hardware developer."

**107**

Jerry's jaw dropped. "You don't develop software?" He read the résumé and looked at his notes.

"Uh-oh," he said, frowning, "we have a problem here." He pushed his notes over to her and sure enough, it said "SOFT-WARE DEVELOPMENT" in block letters next to her name. "Would you excuse me?"

He crossed the cafeteria, picked up a wall phone and dialed. He spoke for a minute or so, then dialed again. He was still frowning when he came back.

"I'm really sorry, Lorie," he said, "but somebody goofed big-time. You're scheduled for seven interviews, all working with computers and programming. I just got you in to talk with Systems Engineering, though, and they're closer to what you want. Look, as long as you're here, why don't you talk with them all and get a feel for the work we're doing."

Lorie swallowed hard, not knowing if the anger or the tears would show first. "Isn't there anything open anywhere in circuit design?"

"Lorie, I'm sorry. Talk with these people today and I'll keep your résumé and get back to you with the first appropriate opening, I promise."

Bell Labs offered Lorie the systems engineering job, plus a special paid program to get her master's degree.

*Recruiters are often not technical. Verify the job you are interviewing for, and if there is a misunderstanding, hang in there anyway. Something could work out.*

# Looking Good

*Clothes make the man.*

Anonymous

It's not exactly that Mike was a slob in college, just that he savored the new sartorial freedom after four years of suit-and-tie-every-day in prep school. He let his hair grow, and rumor said he put his corduroys and casual shirts in a pillow case every night and slept on them.

But he wasn't naïve about the "real world." An engineering student with good grades, Mike wanted to work for a major corporation and knew that cut-off shorts and wrinkled shirts wouldn't do for his campus interviews. He tapped his parents for a wardrobe advance and bought the perfect ensemble: dark pin-striped suit, black wing-tipped shoes, black socks, button-down white shirt and conservative red tie. He even got a neat, business-like haircut.

The day before his morning interviews with all three major car companies, Mike wore his new outfit to test its effect. Friends didn't recognize him, and more than one girl whistled. Yes! He was ready.

But he never thought about Structural Engineering Lab that afternoon. With its layers of fine white dust built up over years of shatter-testing cement blocks, it was the last place anyone should wear a dark suit. People entering that lab soon looked like they'd been dipped in powdered sugar.

Mike realized his mistake quickly, but too late. His suit was covered with cement dust. The more he tried to brush it off, the more he rubbed it in. "Nooooo!" he wailed as he kept brushing.

"Dry cleaning is the only way to get that stuff out, Mike," the sympathetic instructor told him.

"But I have my big interviews tomorrow morning." He was panicking.

"You've still got time. Skip lab and take it right over to the cleaners. Now."

He got there at 4:45 and was relieved to see a "Rush Service Available" sign in the window. The fat man behind the counter didn't make him feel any better when he laughed at the suit and smirked, "What, you work in a bakery or somethin', kid?"

Mike pleaded urgently, "Can you get it clean? By first thing tomorrow morning?"

"Yeah, kid, sure. Take it easy."

**109**

He relaxed a little. "When can I pick it up?"

"Eight am," said the fat man. "We start at six."

That's cutting it close for my 8:30 interview, Mike thought, but what choice do I have? He left the suit.

At exactly 8 o'clock the next morning, Mike got to the cleaners wearing his button-down white shirt, red tie, black socks, winged-tipped shoes...and jogging shorts.

The fat man came around the counter and said, "We have a little problem, kid," and he held up the suit — not stiff as a *board,* stiff as *cement!*

Mike went into a full panic. "The biggest interviews of my life are in a half-hour, and I'm wearing a pair of shorts!"

"I'm sorry, kid, I feel real bad about this," the fat man apologized. "Look, if there's one thing I've got, it's plenty of suits. Pick one that fits, and I'll let you borrow it for today."

Mike didn't like the idea of wearing some stranger's suit, but he had no choice. He rummaged through the rack — the suits were arranged by owner, not size — gathered up six that looked appropriate and tried on three before he found one that "sort of" fit.

He scurried back to campus in the blue suit and made it just on time to his first interview. He did well enough to get a call-back from General Motors, which eventually hired him.

Mike stayed in the automotive industry and his engineering career blossomed. Today, he lives in Grosse Pointe, Michigan where he's known as a sharp dresser.

*If you do avoid a pre-interview disaster, put it out of your mind during the interview and stay focused on getting the job.*

# High Marks

*Thinking is the hardest work there is, which is the probable reason so few people engage in it.*

Henry Ford

When the bottom fell out of the California housing market, Gary, a skilled carpenter, moved to New Jersey for work. He was proud of his knowledge and skills. A portfolio of pictures, including a complicated redwood deck around a geodesic-dome home, testified to the quality of his work.

Gary answered an ad and now sat in the construction trailer at a new home development site with the general contractor, Jack, a muscular man with a deeply suntanned face.

"Nice stuff," Jack admired, looking through the portfolio. "This deck must have been a breaker."

"You bet it was. I'm proud of that one."

"Okay, your work looks good, but before I hire anyone, they take this test," Jack said, pulling some stapled pages out of his desk. "Let's see what you really know. It should take you about 20 minutes."

Gary had never seen a written test for a carpentry job, but why argue? Besides, he was confident of his knowledge. There were 30 questions. In ten minutes he handed them back.

"That was quick. Gave up fast didn't you?" Jack said with a grin.

He pulled out a little handbook and graded the test. "Well I'll be damned. A perfect score. I've given this test a hundred times and still have to look up some of the answers."

"Great," said Gary. "I can start right away. When do you need me?"

"Are you kidding?" Jack replied. "Guys like you I don't need. I want boys who *fail* this test. A smart guy like you, you'll do things your own way, then you'll be telling *me* how to do things, and before I know it, you'll be asking for more money. No way will I hire anyone who aces this test first time around."

Gary couldn't convince him otherwise, and never worked for that contractor.

*Sometimes you really are overqualified.*
*If Michelangelo had needed employment, what a mistake it would have been to take a job as a house painter.*

# Mr. White-Out

*It is generally better to deal by speech than by letter.*

Francis Bacon (1561-1624)

It seems so simple and logical. New graduates do it all the time, especially those with new bachelor's degrees and no particular career field in mind. They'll pursue any job using one résumé. After all, with no business experience to list, their education is as relevant to personnel as it is to public relations, right?

Right. But Frank was different. Cooler, more sophisticated, he was a brand new MBA with a combined marketing/finance major. He didn't know which field he wanted, so he made up *two* résumés, one targeting marketing and one finance, and pursued both.

Well, the season was open on entry level marketing jobs that year, and by the second week in May, Frank ran out of his "marketing" résumé. When he saw the *The Wall Street Journal* ad for *"New MBAs, Fortune 500 Consumer Product Marketing Training Program,"* he wanted to get his name in immediately.

Since this was before the PC/word-processing age of instant electronic revisions, precision was necessary. He laid a "finance" résumé on the kitchen table, put on his glasses and carefully whited out the word "finance" in the job objective, just enough white-out to cover, not enough to puddle up. Then, with the typewriter platen loose, he lined up the bottom-line and word-spacing perfectly and typed in the word "marketing," adjusting the space between each letter to make it fit. It took him six tries and 50 minutes to get it exactly right, but you could hardly see the change on the final product.

And it worked. They called him in for an interview.

"Frank," the interviewer said with a broad smile, picking up the résumé, "this is Class-A work."

"Why, thank you. I did work hard, and the grades are pretty good."

"No, no, your résumé. Only a secretary could tell, and even Sheila wasn't sure. She couldn't resist meddling to see what you whited out to substitute 'marketing.' She scraped it off with a razor blade and found

**112**

'finance'
underneath.
Really, Class-A
work," he said, laugh-
ing. "Are you sure you're getting
into the right field? Ever think
about forgery?" And he laughed
again, putting the résumé down.

Frank just sat there and blushed. He felt stupid, caught, guilty, and could only mumble something about how "The school told us to put down an objective." He was completely derailed, and the interview went badly. Frank didn't get the job.

The worst part about it, looking back, is that he fell totally apart when the interviewer was just having some fun. He wasn't trying to embarrass Frank; he knew all the time what was under the white-out, even before he called Frank in. In a way, he was even being complimentary.

*The interviewer knows you are applying for other jobs and there's no shame in having two career directions. If the interviewer is smiling and friendly, the interview is probably not in jeopardy.*

**113**

# Minor Correction

*There's never time to do it right,*
*but there's always time to do it over.*

Anonymous

The door to Emma's storefront résumé-writing service opened and there stood the most dejected looking man she'd ever seen. "Good morning," she said, as cheerfully as she could. "How can I help you?"

"Good morning," he said with a sigh and a mournful voice. "My name is Payne, Ward Payne. I need some help with my résumé."

He'd been job-hunting for three months, he said, "And do you know, I haven't gotten a single response? I have a good work history and decent experience, too." He handed a copy of his résumé to Emma.

"Well," she said, scanning his background, "I don't know much about managing a child abuse agency, but you certainly appear to be qualified in your field."

"That's what I think, too," Payne said, almost plaintively. "So it must be my résumé. I did it myself," he added, as if apologizing.

"A résumé does need to stand out in today's job market," Emma said. "Yours isn't terrible, but I think there's room for improvement. Let me take a longer look and see if I can come up with some suggestions."

"I'd appreciate your advice," said Payne. "I'll stop in again tomorrow. And please, call me if you have any questions."

He looked so desperate that, as he was leaving, she said, "Cheer up, things are always a little slow in the summer."

Emma completed his résumé the next day and called his office. He'd gone home. She called him there, and a pleasant gentleman answered.

"May I speak to Ward Payne?" she asked.

"I'm sorry," he answered, "but there's no Ward Payne here. What number are you calling?"

"Uh, 555-6806," Emma replied.

"Well, that's this number, but there's nobody here by that name. Whoever he is, he must be looking for a job. I've been getting his calls for a couple of months now."

"Sorry," said Emma, and hung up.

"Well, Mr. Payne," she said when he walked into her shop that

**114**

afternoon, "I think I've figured out your problem."

"You have?" His face lit up.

"I believe so. Take a look at your phone number." She handed him his résumé.

"555-68... Oh. Oh, no! Oh, I didn't!"

"Oh, you did," she said. "You put the wrong number on your résumé."

Emma changed the phone number on his résumé and printed it up. One month later, Ward was happily working at a new job.

When you proofread your résumé,
verify your name, address and phone number.

# Split Personality

*A man cannot be too careful in the choice of his enemies.*

Oscar Wilde

That witch, Francine fumed, reading the Sunday help wanted ad. I'll bet that's my job! She's going to replace me!

She studied the ad, which had only a box number for replies. It's everything I do, she thought, secretary-bookkeeper-customer service, small company, same business, same town. It could have my name on it!

Well, that cuts it, Francine decided. I gotta find out for sure, but I'm outta there no matter what!

She'd been thinking about leaving anyway because the workload kept getting heavier, and the last raise was 18 months ago. And then he brought *her* in! "Her" was the owner's wife, the new office manager, and she was a Class-A, certified bitch, the "boss from hell" if there ever was one.

Francine had *two* résumés made up. One was real — real name, phone number, background, etc. — for a serious job search. The other was a one-shot, bona fide phony she'd use to answer "the ad."

*Charity Hump,* the résumé said — a perfect name, they're taking advantage of me! — was God's gift to an office manager: world-class skills, big company experience, top-drawer education, prominent references. And she works cheap! The address and phone number belonged to her friend, Mandy, who agreed to play along.

I wonder if I'm overdoing it, Francine thought. Nope. She'll call. And the résumé went in the mail to the box number.

"Mrs. Lucifer" did call and invite "Ms. Hump" to interview for the job — Francine's job! Charity/Mandy politely declined in her most upper upper-crust voice, explaining that she had already accepted "a more suitable position" elsewhere.

And for Francine, it was the truth. She got a new job after sending out only five of her real résumés.

*Information on impending layoffs is valuable.*
*If you discover your job is in jeopardy,*
*consider it a head start in finding your next job.*
*You don't have to wait for the ax to fall.*

# Longest Day

*Experience is the name everyone gives to their mistakes.*

Oscar Wilde

Darren reviewed the day so far with a smile of satisfaction: 4 am left home in South Jersey and drove to a helicopter company in Connecticut; 8 am met human resources director who was enthusiastic about him and his "fit" with the engineering job; 9-12 talked with two engineering department heads; 12-1 pleasant lunch in company cafeteria with other engineers; 1-3 met with two more department heads; 3-4 got explanation of company benefits and watched company rah-rah video; and now he was waiting to see the human resources director again, a good sign!

Twelve hours so far, he thought, a real marathon, but worth it. Have another cup of coffee and try to stay awake.

At five, the director finally came in. "Sorry to keep you waiting, Darren, but I couldn't leave that meeting and I wanted to talk to you again."

"No problem," Darren replied, trying not to look bleary.

"I wanted to tell you two things," the director said. "First, everybody you spoke with today was really impressed. Congratulations."

Darren perked up. "Great. Glad to hear it. I was impressed with them, too."

"And second, the official job description finally came in while you were interviewing. Here's a copy for you."

Darren read it and his face fell.

"This is for a production engineer," he said, looking up, puzzled. "I'm a design engineer."

"That's okay, we're not very hung up on titles around here," the director said easily.

"No, you don't understand," Darren continued. "They're completely different. I *design* engines for helicopters. On the computer, mathematical models, new concepts, plans. A production engineer works in the plant helping to put the engines together."

"Well, if you can do one you can do the other, it seems to me," the director said.

"Um, no, not really," said Darren, trying to stay cool. "A design engineer is like an architect; a production engineer is more like a builder. They work together, but frankly, design engineering demands a much higher skill set. If I'd known the job was for a production engineer, I wouldn't have come up."

The director spent ten minutes trying to convince him it was really the same job. Darren just couldn't make him understand. Finally, angry and disappointed, Darren left. Eighteen hours wasted interviewing for a job he wasn't interested in!

It was 10 o'clock by the time he got home, and he was furious all the way. But at least it kept him awake driving home.

*While you're making arrangements for the interview,*
*verify the job you're interviewing for.*

# Say What?

*You can't depend on your eyes
when your imagination is out of focus.*

Mark Twain

Ellen was "blind as a bat" without her glasses and agonizing over it. She was about to do her trial-day of elementary teaching in Fort Worth, Texas, with the school principal observing. I have to be able to see! Getting this first job depends on it.

A solution! She stopped at a drugstore on the way to school and bought a thick black safety cord to attach to her glasses and hang around her neck to keep from losing them. Finally, she felt secure.

Her teaching debut went smoothly. Ellen handled the kids' normal attempts to confuse and mislead a substitute teacher, got control early and even managed to teach the day's lesson plan.

After class, the principal came up from the back of the room, leaned in toward her and shouted, "Very good, Miss Manzo! You'll be hearing from us soon."

Why is he shouting? she thought, we're two feet apart. She decided not to ask. Maybe he spends his life shouting over the kids and doesn't even notice anymore.

A week later, Ellen was rejected. She was disappointed but knew she'd done her best. Eventually, she found a job at a nearby school.

She'd been teaching there for several years when a familiar face appeared in the main office one Monday morning. "Didn't you used to work at an elementary school in Forth Worth?" Ellen asked. "You know, I once tried for a position at that school."

"Yes, I was working there then," the secretary replied. "You almost got that job, too, but the principal was worried how your handicap might affect your teaching."

"Handicap? What handicap?" Ellen asked in amazement.

"Your hearing problem. You had that thick black wire to the hearing aid hidden in your glasses. I guess you wear one that fits in your ear now?"

*If you feel strongly about a job and your performance at the interview was top-notch, find out why they turned you down.*

# Twins

*It is not only fine feathers that make fine birds.*

Aesop

**I**t was 7:30 am on *the* day. This day was going to open whole new vistas for Barry's career as a salesman. At 9 he was interviewing with, in his opinion, the biggest, the best, the most progressive copier company with the broadest line of quality products the world had ever known! And he was going to knock 'em dead!

Showered, shaved and shined, he faced the first decision of the day. What to wear?

Conservative. Got to fit that corporate culture. He picked the single-breasted charcoal-gray pin-stripe.

But I'm a salesman, he thought, not an accountant. Got to project that, too, just a touch of flash to remember me. He chose a freshly starched pale yellow button-down shirt and red-and-gold-striped tie, then the gold ID bracelet and gold-nugget tie tack.

High-top black socks and the new black loafers, casual but sharp, completed the outfit. The shoes gleamed. And the tassels suggested golf. He had a bagful of golf stories.

Barry checked himself at the mirror and was satisfied. Perfect. Go get 'em, tiger. He left the hotel and stepped right into a cab. An omen, he thought, this is *my* day, *my* day.

He arrived three minutes early and was ushered right in to meet Curt, the sales VP.

Barry entered the office. Curt came around the desk. They both stopped short...and erupted. They were dressed exactly alike, exactly — suits, shirts and ties right down to the tasseled loafers and ID bracelets.

"Did you guys plan this?" Curt's secretary chuckled. "Now that's what I call affinity!"

Well, the ice was broken and the interview sailed along from there. When Curt asked the standard question, "Why should I hire you?" Barry answered without hesitation, "You mean besides my great taste in clothes?"

But Curt was a salesman from the old school. He believed the ability to sell was a natural gift that you either had or didn't have. The product itself was secondary. So he picked up a stapler, gave it to Barry and said, "Sell me this stapler."

Barry turned it over in his hand a few times, opened the loading mechanism, closed it and left the office. Thirty seconds later he was back at the doorway and said, "Knock, knock." He got a laugh, and then launched into a 15-minute impromptu sales pitch for the stapler: it'll give you efficiency, Curt, time and money for you, more time to spend with your sales force, no more searching for lost third-sheets of territory reports, no more paper clips; this stapler could revolutionize your work day.

Curt "bought" the stapler, concluded the interview and Barry left for the hotel to pack and return home. The following week he got the job.

A month later, they were having lunch together when Curt asked, "Do you know why I hired you, Barry?"

"Because I'm a great dresser!"

"No. Believe it or not, I interviewed 26 people and hired only two, you and Angela, who has a lot more experience than you. Most of those people sent follow-up thank-you letters, but only you two mailed them the same day we talked. I checked the postmarks. That said something to me about both of you."

Barry smiled. He remembered thinking that day, should I bother or not, and then writing out the note longhand on hotel stationery and swinging by the post office on the way to the airport. Good decision! he thought now. I knew that was my day.

Barry still works for the copier company. Whenever he has a really important sales call, he wears his "Lucky Outfit."

*Dress for success, obviously. And when you're sending a thank-you note, sooner is better than later.*

# Catholic School

*I desire to go to Hell, not to Heaven. In Hell I shall enjoy
the company of popes, kings and princes, but in Heaven
are only beggars, monks, hermits and apostles.*

Niccolò Machiavelli

"**C**ome back when you have five years' experience," they told
me, public and private schools alike. Talk about *Catch 22!* How
do you get experience if they won't hire you in the first place,
even with a Master's degree in remedial reading?

So when I saw the "teacher wanted" ad from a Roman Catholic
school I answered it, even though it was a 40-minute drive from home.
The Mother Superior, also the principal of the school, interviewed me. She
was an older, no-nonsense-type woman still wearing the traditional floor-
length black habit.

"Are you Catholic?" she asked.

Yes, I assured her, but didn't mention that the week before I'd talked
with a Jewish private school, and no one there asked me about my religion.

"What does your husband do for a living?"

"Is that important?" I was a little indignant. She wasn't hiring *him,*
after all. And it was the second illegal question, two of two so far.

"Well, dear," the Mother Superior said, "we don't pay much, and I
must be sure the woman we hire won't leave in the middle of the year for
more money."

"I know the salary, Mother Superior, it was in the ad, and if I sign a
contract, I'll certainly honor it." I didn't point out that it was illegal to consider only women for the job.

She then described some conditions not mentioned in the ad.

"We don't have school buses, you know. Our teachers provide transportation. You'll be assigned three students to pick up and drop off daily."

"Do I get paid extra for that?"

"No," she said flatly.

"Well, gas money then?"

"No," said the nun, and without hesitation, "you'll also be expected
to help drive your athletic team, the one you'll coach every semester, to all
the away games."

**123**

I nodded at that, stunned to silence.

"Also, many of our students are quite poor," the Mother Superior went on, "so the school provides a free lunch."

At last, I thought, a *benefit* to this job. A free lunch.

"Teachers bring in canned food and leftovers from home, and help prepare lunch for the students," she told me.

"But Mother Superior," I said, finally moved to object, "with the low salary, my extra car and insurance expenses, and feeding the students too, I could actually lose money on this job after taxes."

"Well, dear, it is God's work after all."

I decided then that I really wasn't interested in volunteer work. Whoever took that job would have to be teacher, slave and saint rolled into one.

I found a job in another private school and have been a teacher in a public school for the last ten years.

*Experience must often be bought — paying your dues, they say —*
*and compensation for many entry-level jobs is based on that fact.*
*How much you're willing to pay is up to you.*

# On Stage

*Memory, the warder of the brain.*

William Shakespeare, *Macbeth*

The suburban New Jersey school board meeting dragged through the evening in the hot, stuffy auditorium. Nine-thirty, 10 o'clock, 10:30. The handful of parents attending drifted away but Barry waited, struggling to stay interested and alert. His interview for the superintendent of schools position was last on the agenda.

At 10:45, they called him to the stage and asked him to sit on the lone chair at a small table facing the 12 members of the board who were formidably arrayed behind a long, wooden table.

"Good evening, Dr. Singer, and thank you for waiting," the chairwoman said, still chipper despite the hour. "We've all read your *Curriculum Vitae*. Your career is impressive."

"Thank you, thank you very much," Barry replied, a little flattered.

"Perhaps the way to begin," she continued, "is for you to describe your career in chronological order from the time you got your Ph.D."

Barry's mind went blank. *My first job...a private school... teaching history...but when was it exactly...and where in Connecticut?* He couldn't remember. He came prepared to talk about the new issues in education, not to go step-by-step through a 20-year career.

The board members waited expectantly, glancing down at the copies of his *C.V.* in front of them.

Barry took a sip of water and scanned the long table facing him, eyes stopping on the chairwoman.

"I could do that, yes," he said. "But I wonder if that's the best use of the board's time. I believe you have all the details of my career in front of you.

"When I started 20 years ago, schools had money, parents came to board meetings and teachers worried about students chewing gum in class, not about guns in the locker room and drugs in the parking lot. I could tell you what I did 20 years ago, but I'd much rather tell you what I can do now."

He paused, again scanning the board, waiting for their reaction. A few exchanged whispers, a few nodded.

Then, "Please do, Dr. Singer. We'd like to hear your thoughts."

He did, and the rest of the evening went very well indeed, with a lively discussion following his remarks.

After the meeting, the chairwoman took him aside and said, "You won't get the official letter until next week, but unofficially, I can tell you the job is yours."

◎

*An interview is like a chess game.*
*Position yourself in order to have the advantage.*

# Bad Connection

*There is no reason for any individual
to have a computer in their home.*

Ken Olson
President, Digital Equipment Corp.,
Convention of the World Future Society,
Boston, 1977*

Hunt dashed toward the big brokerage house through New York City's worst thunderstorm of the season. Damn, he thought. Only two things could ruin this demo — an electrical surge or a telephone outage — and this storm could do either.

He was after the biggest contract ever for his on-line file server system which would allow their brokers nationwide to dial from their PCs into his remote mainframe database 24-hours a day, and today was demonstration day. The hardware was connected. He was prepared. He was nervous.

Eight top executives entered the conference room. After introductions, coffee and cordial small talk, the senior man said, "Okay, Hunt, let's see how this thing works."

"Yes, sir!" He sat down confidently at the PC.

"Connecting with our computer is the simplest thing in the world. You just select the 'Dial In' option on the main menu and choose our computer access number in the pop-up window — like this."

He punched the key and waited for the modem-connect signal. Nothing happened. "Uh, there might be a bad connection from the storm," he said, frowning. "I'll re-dial direct."

He did. Nothing.

The executives began to fidget, but Hunt refused to panic. "Let me call the office to make sure there's no problem there."

The conference room phone was connected to the PC, so Hunt used his cellular phone. Turning away from the group, he hissed, "Wanda, it's me. What the hell's going on over there? I've got a room full of people and I can't get into the system!"

"Everything's up here, boss. Must be on your end."

---

*Cerf, C. and Navasky, V. *The Experts Speak: The Definitive Compendium of Authoritative Misinformation*, Pantheon Books, 1984, p. 209.

Hunt turned back to the group. "Well, we should be okay now. I'll dial in again."

Nothing. I'm screwed! he moaned to himself. Screwed!

The brokerage chief said, "Look, Hunt, we haven't got all day. I'll get our PC expert over from the other building to take a look at it."

Billy arrived a few minutes later, soaked from the storm still raging outside, and no more than twenty years old. Hunt was annoyed that they'd brought in this kid to second-guess him.

The top man explained what was happening, or not happening, and without asking, Billy sat down at the PC terminal. "Is this your phone number on the screen?" he asked.

"Yes," replied Hunt impatiently. He *didn't* add "What a stupid question, you smug little weasel."

"Then that's your problem," said Billy. "You gotta dial '9' to get an outside line." Billy re-dialed and the connection was made. He got up and left.

Hunt finished his demonstration, but the executives weren't paying much attention and asked no questions. Filing out, he heard one whisper, "He expects to get an on-line system contract, and he can't even dial a phone?"

*If you're doing a demo, do a trial run before the audience arrives.*

# The End

*Rudeness is the weak man's imitation of strength.*

Eric Hoffer

**B**ruce was a textbook example of the "little-man syndrome" — small stature, big ego, super-aggressive. He'd booked the paneled conference room to interview the new kid for the entry-level accounting job and "impress the hell out of him," without exposing his own tiny office.

He met "the kid," Al, in the lobby at 2 pm and ushered him into the building, strutting all the way to Conference Room A. A very young secretary guarded the door.

"Sorry, Renee, this is mine, it's booked. Find someplace else, okay?"

Renee didn't move. Hesitantly, lower lip quivering, she mumbled, "You can't go in. Mr. Fisher's in there."

His authority challenged, Bruce exploded. "Damn it, Renee, I'm sick of this! Every day, Fisher takes over an entire conference room to eat his lunch and read the paper. This is booked. Get him the hell out of there."

"I can't," she wailed, and broke into hysterical tears, completely startling Bruce. Not good for his career if anyone thought he was abusing secretaries.

"Take it easy, calm down, Renee, it's okay. We'll get some coffee and come back in a few minutes when Fisher's gone. Calm down, but get him out, okay?"

"You don't understand," she sobbed, "Mr. Fisher isn't coming out. He's dead!"

Bruce shoved past her into the conference room and Al followed. Sure enough, there was Mr. Fisher, stretched out cold, white and still on the long oak table, surrounded by overstuffed leather chairs.

Back in the corridor, Al distinctly heard Bruce mutter, "Oh, hell. Now I'll have to interview you in my office." And he did, irritably, for a full hour.

It did not go well.

*Some interviews are dead on arrival—beyond resurrection.*

Chapter 5

# Unexpected People

# Legal Brief

*He said enough. Enough said.*

Gertrude Stein

Now I ask you, how would you feel?

You commute three hours a day from Connecticut to a paralegal job in downtown Manhattan, drive a battered Plymouth and eat peanut butter sandwiches three nights a week to save money for law school. And you have a boss just out of Harvard Law who orders his lunch in French, plays squash, spends his weekends in the Hamptons, drives a Ferrari, has "future partner" written all over him....and is patronizing as hell about it! How would you feel?

Me too. I hated Stanley's guts!

So when I saw the ad for a paralegal in a manufacturing company just 15 minutes from home, at about the same money with all benefits, including tuition reimbursement, *and no Stanley,* I jumped at it.

And I got an interview.

I talked with the personnel director first and knew right away I was golden with him. He liked my qualifications, and I could talk his language. They manufactured construction cable and chain. My father worked for Bridgeport Brass, so I tossed off a few intelligent remarks about alloys and tensile strength. He gobbled it up.

The personnel guy took me up to their general counsel. He was a big man, 50-ish, with a wrinkled brown suit, huge hands and a wide, welcoming grin. "Happy to meet you, Gene, come on in, I'm just making coffee. Have a doughnut. Yeah, I like those little cream-filled suckers too. By the way, call me Bob."

Now here's an unpretentious guy, I thought. He probably had to really scratch to get where he is. What a difference from Stanley!

We sat down at a scarred conference table littered with papers and books and he said, "Okay, Gene, here's the skinny. I'm up to my neck here. I gotta draw all our contracts, research and file our environmental statements, keep the SEC, EPA and OSHA happy and deal with a bunch of Fairfield County lawyers outta Yale who eat cucumber sandwiches on Sunday afternoons.

"I'm all alone so you'd report directly to me. It's a big workload, but we pay time-and-a-half for overtime. Plus, there's a fair amount of travel around the state, so we have a company car available. How's it sound?"

"You want the truth?" I said. "Fabulous! I can help you, really get into all that for you. I already know something about metals and the construction industry. And I'd sure like working for you."

In fact, I was so excited I took a big swig of hot coffee and burned my tongue.

**133**

Bob finished his coffee and sprawled back in his chair. "Good. So tell me, Gene, why are you looking to leave where you are now? That's a good firm."

I sat back too, confident and expansive. "That's true, it's a great firm and I'm learning a lot there. And Manhattan's a really with-it place. But there's the commute. And taxes.

"And frankly, Bob, I hate my boss's guts." Mentally, I flipped Stanley a great big bird. "He's a snotty little rich kid, *Haa-vud Law* and all that, and he never lets me forget it. I can't stand those bluebloods. I mean, just because *his* daddy could send him to *Haa-vud* to study torts with some doddering old, you should excuse me, some doddering old farts, I mean, just because his snooty *Haa-vud* buddies put him right on the partnership track doesn't mean he's any better than me, right? I'm no dope, you know."

The interview ended shortly after that. Bob mentioned something vague about a decision in the next few weeks and, I wasn't sure why, he seemed to get more formal.

Then as I was leaving his office I saw them. Grouped and prominently displayed on the wall by the door: a Harvard plaque and, on either side of it, framed Harvard undergraduate and law degrees. I felt like a complete and total fool.

"Thanks for coming, Gene," he said from behind me. "I'm sure you're smart enough to find your own way out. And incidentally, Harvard has a wonderful scholarship program." All I could do was nod.

The rejection letter arrived three days later.

*Learn something about your interviewer by looking around the room at pictures, diplomas and memorabilia. A common interest can enhance an interview.*

*Think positive, talk positive, be positive. Negative thoughts, words or attitudes have no place at an interview.*

# Shovel or Gun

*Goo-o-o-o-o-o-o-d morning, Vietnam!*

*Good Morning, Vietnam,* 1987 film

J im was 21, and with a fresh haircut and brand new B.S. in computer science, he was on his way to the first job interview of his life.

The warm, sunny afternoon crossing the Jersey marshes in early summer 1965 turned dark and smelly as the bus entered the Lincoln Tunnel to Manhattan. *Not an omen, I hope. Nah, Larry at the employment agency told me I'm perfect for this job, close as it gets to a sure thing.* Still, Jim was nervous.

The bus arrived at the Port Authority Terminal with a whooosh of air brakes, and he took the escalator to the main concourse. He politely refused literature from the Black Panthers, Students for a Democratic Society, Youth International Peace Party, Jehovah's Witnesses, Young Republicans and the Jewish Defense League — skirted the white-sheeted Hare Krishna's clanking their cymbals and tambourines — and exited onto Eighth Avenue, right into a group of middle-aged women brandishing placards reading NOT OUR SONS, NOT YOUR SONS, NOT THEIR SONS. The escalating Vietnam War aroused strong passions.

Jim squeezed by the crowd and set off for his interview. He spent a half-hour there filling out forms on a clipboard, and finally got to see the owner of the mid-sized manufacturing company.

"Come in, come in, glad to see you, Jim," he was greeted with a hearty handshake. "Have a seat and give me a minute with this, okay?" Dave, the owner, sat behind his huge glass-topped desk and flipped through Jim's application.

His smile disappeared. He punched the intercom button on his phone. "Jennifer, get me Larry over at the agency."

"Is something wrong?" Jim asked, sensing surely there was but without a clue what it might be.

Gruffly, the owner assured him, "Nothing to do with you, Jim, it's these damned agency people. Never get anything straight."

"Larry's on line one."

"Thanks, Jennifer." He punched the lighted button. "Hello, Larry? What the hell are you trying to pass off on me? Are you an idiot or do you think I am?" Jim's stomach flopped. *This was not a good sign.*

"Larry, he's single, no dependents, good health, no military service, not even in the reserves! I told you, I only want to see men classified as 'unfit for military service.' Get with it, Larry. Don't pull this on me again or I'll find a new agency!" He slammed the receiver back into its multi-buttoned cradle.

"Jim, I'm sorry," he said, and he seemed genuinely so, "but I'll be damned if I'll spend another nickel training someone to have the army snap him up. Your situation gives you only two options, Jim — digging ditches until you're drafted because no one else will hire you, or killing Vietcong — take your choice, a shovel or a gun."

Eight months later, Jim was drafted into the Marines. Of the 80 men in his platoon from basic training, 78 became infantrymen in Vietnam; one became a data processing specialist stationed in Florida; and Jim became a supply clerk stationed in North Carolina, half a world away from the front-lines in Southeast Asia. Today, Jim owns a software consulting company.

◉

*Despite the law, candidates today still get rejected*
*for political, racial and religious prejudices.*
*You can fight it or move on.*

# Party Phone

*I drink only to make my friends seem more interesting.*

Seumas MacManus

"Hey, buddy, Kevin here. Pizza and a keg at my place Friday night, okay? Come early and stay late. Pass the word. See ya." He left the same message on all his friends' answering machines.

Kevin lived in a "singles" apartment — The Party House, they called it — on a little lake in Ypsilanti, Michigan and worked in the finance department at General Motors in Detroit. But not for much longer, he hoped. He was just one of a crowd of MBAs there and wanted to move ahead to a small or mid-size company where he could be noticed. He'd been answering job ads nationwide for three or four months.

By 9:30 Friday, though, he wasn't thinking about a new job. The party was in high gear, and Kevin, with more than a few beers down already, was much more interested in the leggy redhead at the CD changer. Who is *that*, he was wondering when the phone rang. Still ogling the redhead, he answered it.

"Daniels here."

"Mr. Daniels? This is Mitch Anderson of Anderson Manufacturing in New Haven, Connecticut. You sent us a résumé in response to our ad in *The Wall Street Journal* for a financial manager. Say, did I catch you at a bad time?"

"No, not at all, I, uh, I just have a few friends over. Can you hold on a minute while I switch to another phone?"

He punched the Hold button and elbowed his way into the bedroom, evicting a couple who were getting to know each other better, and closed the door. It shut out most of the noise.

"Uh, Mr. Anderson?"

"Are you sure this isn't a bad time? I could get back to you."

Jeez, he thought, should I tell this guy I'm too fulla beer now to talk business? He'd never call back. Besides, how do you say, Look, I'm sorry, could you call back when I'm sober? Definitely unprofessional! He giggled at the thought.

"No, no, really, it's fine, no problem."

"Well, I liked your résumé, Kevin, and I'd like to hear a little more about you. What attracted you to the position described in our ad?"

**137**

Kevin closed his eyes and tried desperately to think. He must have answered a hundred ads in the past few months, and drunk or sober, he couldn't remember Anderson Manufacturing. Luckily, he was at his desk where he kept all the ads he'd answered in the top drawer. He searched through the drawer frantically. Meanwhile, he stalled.

"Well, uh, you see — it's Mr. Anderson, isn't it? — well, Mr. Anderson, I've always been interested in your type of business, and of course your company has a great reputation in the industry." Whatever industry *that* might be, he thought, still searching.

*There it is! Anderson Manufacturing!* He pounced on the ad and read:

> WANTED — hands-on financial manager with good people skills, general ledger experience, excellent verbal and presentation skills. Works well under tight deadlines.

"And how would you describe yourself, Kevin?"

"Well," he said, holding the ad up to the light and mentally crossing his fingers, "I'm a hands-on type, really like to be involved, you know? I'd say I have good people skills, and I enjoy presentations. Tight deadlines don't bother me, I know general ledger inside out and people say my verbal skills are pretty good."

And if you have your ad in front of you, I'm finished, he added to himself, but at this hour, you're probably calling from home and the ad's back at the office. He held his breath.

The beer gods were with him. Mr. Anderson responded enthusiastically, "Terrific! That's exactly the type of person I'm looking for. You know, I think it might be worthwhile if the two of us...."

Kevin never found out what might be worthwhile for the two of them.

At that moment, someone picked up the kitchen phone, giggling loudly, and shouted, "Hey Daniels, you friggin asshole! Get off the phone, will ya? The keg just ran dry! You're the host, goddammit, and we're all drunk. Go out and get some more beer!"

The unidentified drunk slammed the phone back on the hook, and there was total silence on the line.

"Uh, look, Mr. Anderson," Kevin mumbled weakly, "I, uh, I think maybe we should...."

"I guess I really did call at a bad time," Mr. Anderson stated coldly. "I'll talk to you again after the weekend. Good night, Mr. Daniels." He hung up.

The next week came and went with no call. Kevin got Anderson Manufacturing's phone number, but could never catch Mr. Anderson in. He left messages, but they were never returned.

**138**

*First impressions last forever. It's okay to defer
an unplanned telephone interview, especially on a Friday night.*

# Stand-Up

*Laugh and the world laughs with you.*

Ella Wheeler Wilcox, *Solitude,* 1883

Comedy was Roger's favorite pastime through college and law school. He loved the classic comedians — Milton Berle, Jackie Gleason, Jimmy Durante, George Burns, Steve Allen. They had style, something modern comics lacked. Roger even did his own little stand-up routines on "open-mike" nights at the new comedy clubs springing up.

But he never let comedy interfere with schoolwork. Excellent grades at a famous Eastern law school won him an interview with a large, well known Philadelphia law firm.

It was certainly an "old money," Main Line firm. The office decor was rich, traditional ... and dark. Everything was dark — dark wood paneling, dark leather chairs, dark carpeting, dark draperies, dark paintings on the walls. Dark. And depressing!

It was also quiet as a library. Nobody spoke above a whisper and the telephones rang with a single muted ding. It was geriatric, each partner he talked with older than the last. And it was warm, extremely warm. Old people always seem to like it warm, he thought.

The darkness, quiet and warmth combined to make Roger feel there was a serious chance he'd fall asleep every time he sank into one of the soft leather chairs in a partner's office. He accepted coffee every time it was offered.

Finally, in late afternoon, Roger was ushered in to meet the senior partner himself. Three other partners accompanied him into the very large office. The head of the firm, a grandfatherly type, puffed contentedly on a pipe, tobacco smoke pungent in the air.

After introductions, Roger was directed to "the client's chair" directly in front of the old man's massive desk. The others melted silently away to the edges of the room.

The senior partner leaned forward and asked, "Well, Roger, what's your impression of the firm?"

That was a straight-line from Heaven!

All day, Roger had been trying to sort out his mixed feelings about the firm, and this did it. The lawyer in him cringed, the comedian exulted.

He stood up, slowly scanning the entire room, and in his best stand-up voice intoned...

"What's my *impression?* What's my *impression?* Why...*I don't DO impressions.* But thank you, thank you, thank you. You've been a *wonderful* audience." With a long sweep of the arm, he bowed low to the flabbergasted senior partner, turned and swept out of the office and the firm.

At least now I know what I'm cut out for, he chuckled on the way home.

Today Roger represents a European toy company and lives a decidedly upscale life in London and Belgium.

*Doing what you do well is good;*
*doing well what you love is what life is all about.*

**141**

# Sense of Humor

*Many friends have been lost by jest, but few have been gained.*

Anonymous

Gentlemen, your new manager of corporate planning: Larry Henderson! Yeah!

Leaving his fifth interview with the big non-profit health insurance carrier, Larry was sure they'd offer it to him now. These folks want to change, get really customer-friendly, and I'm the guy to do it for 'em. They as much as told me so today. This company's going places, and I'm going with it!

For Larry, a freewheeling consultant, this was his golden opportunity — reorganize a major firm that had grown fat, happy and bureaucratic over the years and draw a regular, big-bucks paycheck twice a month too. Plus the benefits and perks. Yes! He took his wife out to dinner that night.

The next morning, tearing yesterday's page off his *Far Side* cartoon desk calendar, he stopped short, gaped at it a moment and laughed out loud.

A 747 jetliner was taking off from an airport near a swamp dragging a big old bullfrog along with it. Mistaking the plane for a smaller, more edible flying object, the frog had shot its tongue out to capture it, and got stuck to the plane. There was this frog, tongue latched to the jet's fuselage, zooming skyward with an astonished look on its face.

That frog is me, he thought, the plane is the company, and we're both taking off to new heights. Prophetic. And funny, too. He liked it so much that he faxed copies to each of the people he'd interviewed with, from the personnel director right up to the president, along with a note explaining how he felt.

He expected at least a couple of calls about it, but nothing. For five whole days, nothing. On the sixth day, he got a letter saying they'd promoted somebody from inside the company.

Larry was convinced the cartoon cost him the job.

"I should have realized," he said to his wife. "Nobody had any sense of humor there. I thought it was funny; they must've thought it was weird."

"Maybe they just don't like frogs," his wife sympathized.

**142**

*Jobs have been lost by jest; few have been gained.*

# Sneakers

*A worker is, first of all, a person who must fit into
the social community in which he works.*

Guy Wadsworth,
National Industrial Conference Board, 1941

Adam, a computer consultant who worked in Manhattan, had adopted two New York traditions. He didn't own a car, and he wore comfortable sneakers walking to work, carrying his business shoes to put on when he arrived.

Well, during a long dry spell between assignments, with no cash at all coming in, Adam decided to give up consulting and find "a real job," as he told his friends. He contacted a recruiter.

"I'm biting the bullet," he told her, a thirty-something woman named Midge. "Living from job to job is too uncertain. I need a salaried position."

"Your creditors will bless you for that," Midge said.

Within a couple of weeks, she got him an interview with a multibillion dollar company in Westchester County, about 50 miles north of the city. On the day of the interview he overslept, waking with barely enough time to gulp down a cup of coffee, struggle into his suit and sneakers, grab his briefcase and catch the train at Grand Central Station.

This commute could be a drag, he thought, watching the landscape rattle by the windows of the Metro North car. The trip took about an hour, and then another 15 minutes to walk from the station to the company's headquarters. In the lobby he asked for the men's room to exchange sneakers for shoes.

Opening the briefcase, he found six résumés and a pen, a calculator, an address book, a pair of black socks...but no shoes. You blew it, buddy, he told the reflection in the mirror; Midge won't be proud.

Looking down at his feet, he knew nobody could mistake those old Adidas for anything but old Adidas. He sighed. Okay, he thought, closing the briefcase with a snap, what's done is done. I came here to interview, so that's what I'll do. And he left the lavatory with a determined, self-confident stride. If the subject of shoes comes up, he told himself, make a clever remark, explain what happened and carry on as best you can.

He signed in at the front desk, got his visitor's badge and settled down to wait for the personnel associate he was to see.

On the dot of 10, a small, impeccably dressed man appeared. He had rimless glasses, short hair brushed close to his head and almost no chin. Very uptight, Adam thought.

"Mr. Prescott?" Adam asked. "Good morning, I'm..."

"Yes," said Mr. Prescott in a nasal voice. He shook Adam's hand for a brief, limp moment. "Adam Hunt, isn't it? Welcome to..." He glanced down, and his lips compressed into a thin line.

Adam winced internally. "Oh, the sneakers," he said. "I hope they won't get me off on the wrong foot, will they? Heh, heh."

The line of Mr. Prescott's lips became thinner.

"Really, though, I walked to the train in New York and up here from the station," Adam explained. "And I was in such a hurry to get here this morning that I forgot my shoes."

"I see," said Mr. Prescott with a stony stare. "You walked rather than take a cab."

"That's right," Adam said. "I like to walk."

The idea of anyone preferring to walk seemed totally alien to Mr. Prescott.

"Well, let's go inside."

The interview lasted about a half-hour, and Adam knew he had no chance when Mr. Prescott said, "We'll be in touch with you, Mr. Hunt."

Midge confirmed his opinion the next day. "Your Mr. Prescott called me," she told him. "He dressed me down something fierce for sending him someone in sneakers. Said he didn't want to see any more hippies."

"Hippies!" Adam said, hurt.

"Yes, hippies, that's what he said. He told me his boss looked in and you embarrassed him in your sneakers. Pack your bag the night before, Adam."

"Yeah. And make sure my wing-tips are in there, right?"

"Right," Midge said, laughing. "Then you'll be a shoe-in!"

◉

*Lifestyle mismatches can make for a horrible working relationship; don't sweat all the jobs you lose.*

# Witness for the Prosecution

*Anyone who thinks there is good in everyone
hasn't interviewed enough people.*

Anonymous

*They called him Baby Face in college. And his face
was young, sweet, innocent. Now, interviewing with
a telecommunications company for his first job as a
computer analyst, Kevin was afraid his youthful
appearance might be a drawback.*

hat's this, Kevin wondered as a secretary led him into the conference room. Three men sat on one side of the long table, a fourth chair empty, legal pads in front of each. They stared silently as he sat in the single chair opposite them. Wow, he thought, talk about intimidating!

Then the center man stood up and smiled. "Kevin, welcome. I hope you don't mind, but we all wanted to talk with you and it saves time this way." He introduced the others and said, "Charley will be in as soon as he's free."

Kevin thought the interview was going well despite the formidable arrangement. They were talking CD-ROMs when the door opened and an older man walked in — Charley.

As they shook hands, Charley's eyes suddenly bulged and his smile turned ugly. He jumped back and jabbed a finger in Kevin's face. "You!" he shouted. "You're the one! You're the one who raped that girl nine years ago! You went to prison!"

Kevin was dumbstruck. What is this, some kind of test to see how I react? He looked to the others, and their embarrassment told him it wasn't. But they just sat there and said nothing. Stay calm, he told himself, be logical.

"No, I'm sorry, it wasn't me. Nine years ago I was fifteen and in high school."

"You're lying! It's you!"

**147**

Now Kevin was getting upset. "No, it's not. What was his name, this rapist?"

"It was Peter, Peter something," Charley stammered, a little more reasonably. "I can't remember his last name."

Kevin felt that his instincts were paying off and he could return the situation to normal. *"My* name is Kevin," he said calmly. "It wasn't me."

*"That's a lie!"* The crazy man was shouting again, screaming. "You're lying! About your name! Your age! Who you are! It's you! *You* raped that woman!"

Kevin looked to the other men, appealing to them, but they stayed sitting and silent.

It's no use, he thought. "Gentlemen, enough. I don't think I could work here. Thanks, but no thanks." And he walked out.

One of the managers who'd sat there through the entire incident called two weeks later and offered him a job — no mention at all of what had happened, just a job offer. He turned it down.

Kevin did get a job with another telecommunications company, and heard six months later that Charley went home for lunch one day and never came back. No one seemed to know what happened to him.

*If you are denied a job because of false words spoken (slander) or written (libel), you have recourse; consider seeing an attorney.*

# Death Row

*Nothing is as good as it seems beforehand.*

George Eliot, *Silas Marner,* 1861

"**B**ond brokerage boutique" the ad said. In other words, Steve knew, "really small." But he felt lucky to get this interview. In 1991 the big Wall Street firms weren't hiring, they were laying off brokers, and Steve, a junior college finance instructor in South Florida, desperately wanted to be a broker.

Excitement gripped him as he walked in. Telephones ringing. Rows of desks jammed together. Men in telephone headsets hunched over, dialing, talking, fingers flying over keyboards, computer monitors changing like kaleidoscopes. Yes! Not the classroom theory he'd been teaching, the real thing! Action! The brokerage business!

Steve's enthusiasm retreated somewhat when he met Wally, a principal of the firm. Short, thin to the point of anorexia and a chain smoker, he wore an expensive plaid suit, pink shirt, gold bracelets and more rings than anyone could fit on ten fingers — a street-tough, intimidating, transplanted New Yorker. They clashed instantly.

Wally closed the door to his glassed-in office and ostentatiously blew smoke at the No Smoking sign. Steve felt like he'd asphyxiate. After ten hostile minutes, Wally ended the interview. "Nah, kid, you're not the type I want. I need a hustler. You got too much education and you never sold nuttin."

"I don't see how an education in finance hurts in selling financial instruments," Steve objected.

That only drew a look of disgust from Wally. "Yeah, sure. You can find your own way out, cantcha?"

A week later, Steve read that stress interviews were common on Wall Street and thought, okay, why not? What's to lose? He called Wally and said he really wanted to work there.

"Great," Wally enthused, to Steve's astonishment. "Come in Monday, and we'll fix ya up."

Monday came and Steve got a desk almost in the hallway by the copy and fax machines. Associates who sold the most bonds got desks by the windows. The less you sold, the farther from the windows you sat. The last row was called "Death Row" because the next step was out the door, and all new sales associates started there. At least it was convenient to the bathroom.

**149**

The staff included a recovered drug addict and an active alcoholic. Total sales by every associate were posted daily on a giant chalk board. Communication was by screaming, motivation by intimidation.

Periodically, Wally brought the associates into his office for an oral math test, figuring percentages and interest rates quickly in their heads. A wrong answer brought screams or pens and paper clips thrown at your head.

Steve hated it all. But what bothered him most was selling only high-risk, high-commission bonds to retirees. The customer's financial needs didn't matter, only the size of the commission.

Steve never did get off Death Row, and finally quit after three months. He went to work for his father selling kitchen cabinets. His father yelled sometimes too, but at least the cabinets and the relationship were solid.

*Sometimes a stress interview is, in fact, an interviewer's tool*
*to assess your behavior in high-pressure situations.*
*And at other times it's a preview of what the job will be like.*

# Old Guy

*Run for your life!*

Anonymous

Dean knew he'd be the new marketing vice president when Bill McGraff who owned the small sports equipment manufacturing firm invited him for an early morning run. Hadn't he said, "I like to talk with my executives outside the office, you really get to know someone while you're running"?

I'm 35 and in good shape, Dean thought. I jog two or three miles after body building workouts. And he has to be over 60. No sweat.

They met in the park, and Dean suppressed a smile as McGraff stripped off his warm-up suit. The old man looks like a stick, he thought.

"Let's take the outer road," McGraff said. "It's about four miles around."

Well, a little longer than I planned, thought Dean, but no problem. "Sure, why not?"

They started out leisurely and talked marketing, and Dean was enjoying it. Until they reached *The Hill*. I'm supposed to *run* up that? he thought. He did, reduced to nods and grunts as McGraff chatted away. On the down-slope, he recovered enough to pant "Very pretty" as they passed a family of deer grazing in an open field.

Finally, Dean gave up all conversation and concentrated on the run. He broke into a broad smile when their starting point came in view. McGraff didn't slow down. "First four miles, Dean," he shouted. "Three more circuits to go!"

Three more times around? That's another 12 miles!

Halfway through the second lap, McGraff said, "Here, Dean, you'll do better if I pace you. Stay directly behind and match me stride for stride. It's easier that way."

It was humiliating, following behind those spindly 60-year-old legs, pumping away like they could run forever. But it was easier. Maybe he even could make 16 miles.

And then *The Hill* again. He struggled up, seeing spots and gasping for air, but eked over the top and down the other side. At the parking lot, McGraff said, "Why don't you rest a bit? If you don't mind, I'd like to take the last two laps a little faster."

No argument here, Dean thought, and sprawled on a bench as McGraff lengthened his stride and disappeared. By the time he came around on the final circuit, Dean was sitting up and believing that *maybe* he'd be able to walk again...someday.

"Don't look so depressed, Dean. You did 8 miles. That's great for a man with your build."

"I feel like a weakling."

"Why? Because you're not a world-class runner? That's not why I want to hire you. Walk with me while I cool out, and we'll talk salary. And when you're my marketing vice president, Dean, don't ever underestimate the competition."

Dean got an office across from McGraff's, and when both doors were open, he could see the glass case filled with trophies, medals and ribbons the old man had been winning for half a century.

*Whether the interview is in the office or outside,*
*you will find yourself in a situation in which*
*the interviewer is very comfortable. You will be assessed*
*either on your comfort level in that environment*
*or your ability to adapt to it.*

# Bad Chemistry

*I am dying without the help of too many physicians.*

Alexander the Great

**D**amn air conditioning! On the hottest day of the year. It figures. "Milly, what have I got this afternoon? Can I bug out?"

"I regret to inform you, Madam Vice President, that you have a 4:30 interview with Number One on your short list of wannabe administrative assistants – Rhonda. But go home, Shannon, really. I'll reschedule."

"Milly, when duty calls, give your all. I have chosen to set a shining example of suffering along with the troops. Please be sure everyone notes it. I'll stay and sweat with everybody else. Is there anything cold to drink out there?"

The afternoon went by. Slowly.

At 4:30, Milly ushered in a well-dressed, attractive, poised and perfumed young lady — Rhonda.

"Come in and have a seat, Rhonda, please. Milly, would you close the door? I apologize for the air conditioning, or lack of it, but they try to keep us humble sometimes. What a scorcher!"

"Oh, that's OK, It doesn't bother me. You know, I really like the heat."

And indeed Rhonda did seem comfortable. Everyone else was rumpled and red-faced; she looked like a New England autumn. That's good, Shannon thought, unflappable. But that perfume! Wow!

As Shannon picked up the résumé and started to speak...ah choo! Sudden, violent, out of nowhere.

"Bless you!" said Rhonda.

"Oh, thanks," Shannon gasped, reaching for a tissue. I don't know where that came from. "I...uh, ah CHOO!"

Rhonda blinked. "Are you okay?"

"Well, I was a minute ago. Whoo! Would you mind opening the door? I think I need some air in here."

"Of course," and Rhonda hastened to comply.

Shannon's eyes were watering so badly she could hardly see. She wiped them but it didn't help. Her sinuses felt like lead. A summer cold, she thought, a quick and nasty one. Gamely, she carried on.

Then she couldn't breathe. In a minute, she was gasping painfully. Shannon completed the interview quickly and showed Rhonda out with an apology. She had no recollection of what was said.

Worried about her breathing, that something was seriously wrong, she called a doctor in the building who agreed to see her immediately. Down the hall and up in the elevator, she was in his office three minutes later. And the symptoms were gone. She felt fine.

The doctor examined her thoroughly and said, "Shannon, I think you had a severe allergic reaction. It was probably the perfume. You said it was strong."

"But I've never had a reaction to perfume before."

"Well, I suppose it could have been something else. She might have a dog or a cat at home, dander on her clothes. It could be her soap, or her shampoo or her hair spray. There's really no way to tell."

Shannon was fully recovered when she left the doctor's office, and showed no signs of a cold all week. Her remaining interviews went off without a hitch.

"So," asked Milly, "decision time, have you made it?"

"Yup," said Shannon.

"Rhonda? She was the best qualified, and she'd certainly fit in here. I liked her."

"Nope, can't do it. I only remember sneezing when she was here. How can I call and say, Rhonda, I'd like to talk to you again, but this time, don't wear any perfume or hair spray, wash with a different soap, wear different clothes, and if you have a dog or cat, don't bother. How can I do that, Milly? She thinks I'm nuts already."

"Poor Rhonda."

"Right, poor Rhonda. Chalk her off to bad chemistry. Tell me, what'd you think about Joyce?"

◎

*If the most memorable part of the interview is your aroma,*
*you're either wearing too much cologne or you need a shower (or both).*

# Yellow Pad

*Put it in writing.*

AT&T commercial aimed at a competitor

Evelyn was 18 and eager. She wanted to be a secretary at a big corporation — lots of people around, excitement, things happening. But when she got to the interview address, it was upstairs over a coffee shop, file folders crammed in wire baskets along the walls, and what she described as "a nasty, aggressive old hag" greeted her with, "Let's see your résumé."

"I don't have a résumé," Evelyn answered. In the late 1960s secretaries typically didn't; they took typing and shorthand tests.

"I need a résumé," the crone snapped, handing her a yellow pad and fat marking pen. "Go write one out now. Over there."

Evelyn took another look around and politely said, "No, thank you, I don't think so," and walked out.

*The root of a bad interview can be a personality conflict.*
*Better to find out sooner than later. But, just in case*
*the chemistry is right, bring a pen to the interview.*

# Power Play

*The most important thing I have ever learned about management is that the work must be done by other men.*

Alfred P. Sloan, Jr.

**G**ary admired the view: the 5'11" secretary who looked and dressed like a fashion model leading him into the sales vice president's office. Now that's class, he thought.

The corner office wasn't too shabby either — very large, lots of windows, original oil paintings, antique furniture, plush carpet.

But what the hell...? The VP's desk and chair sat on a platform in the middle of the room, 12 inches above everything and everybody else.

"Gary, come in," the VP boomed from on high, phone at his ear. "I'm on hold. Should be off in a few minutes. Have a seat."

"Thanks, but is there a Men's Room I could use?"

"Through that door. I have one in the office here because I make a lot of people so nervous they need it." The trace of a grin appeared.

Still on the phone when Gary came out, the VP totally ignored him for 30 minutes while the phone conversation continued. Gary noted a small conference table in the corner and decided to change the power structure when the VP finally got off the phone.

"Can we sit over there? It'll make conversation more informal."

The VP seemed surprised but agreed. When he came down off the platform, Gary saw, he was actually a chubby little man, no more than 5'6" but all puffed up.

They sat and he stared at Gary. Then, "Why the hell did you use a recruiter? If we do hire you, it'll cost us a fortune."

A tactic, Gary thought. He wants to see how I react. So he replied calmly, "Actually, that was the company's decision. The job wasn't advertised, only recruiters knew about it."

The VP ignored that and charged on. "Why did you get fired from your old company? They must have considered you 'dead wood' or they wouldn't have canned you."

Again, Gary kept his cool and patiently explained about his old company's financial problems and the massive layoffs.

The grilling continued for a half-hour — every question an accusation, no answer good enough. Often, the VP didn't even give him time to

answer one before hitting him with the next.

Suddenly, the VP's attitude changed completely. He leaned back in his chair and pronounced in a friendly voice with a big smile, "If you have time, Gary, I'd like you to meet our president."

"Certainly, I'd like that," replied a surprised Gary.

"Good. I'll have Elaine bring you some coffee while I see if he's available." The VP took Gary's résumé and left, and the gorgeous secretary served him coffee and biscuits on real bone china.

He'd just about finished when the VP was back. "The president can see you now, Gary. Elaine will take you up. Nice to have met you."

The president of the company turned out to be exactly the opposite — tall, thin and athletic, easy going and laid back. His furniture was utilitarian, tables and walls covered with production schedules and engineering drawings.

"Pleased to meet you, Gary," he said with a warm handshake, "you come highly recommended."

They talked easily for ten minutes before the president excused himself to go to a production meeting. "I'm sure you'll be hearing from us real soon."

The recruiter called Gary the next day to say he'd been offered the job. Gary turned it down. The recruiter, of course, was furious. "They loved you. Why would you possibly want to turn them down?"

"Look, I'm not into power games," replied Gary. "The job reports directly to that peacock of a vice president. All day, every day, I'd have to put up with his nonsense. Not me. When I go into a place, I want to do the best job I can, no games."

*In a rapid-fire, stress-type interview with frequent interruptions, the interviewer is assessing your ability to handle heated situations and keep your cool.*

# Constructive Criticism

*MBA in fact stands for 'Massive Business Arrogance.'*
Anonymous

Larry had the world by the tail: 44 years old, retired as a Lt. Colonel with pension guaranteed, still ramrod straight, a shine on his shoes and spring in his step. He'd spent the last 20 years successfully putting organization, training and development problems right for the U.S. Army. With his MBA from Stanford, he was prime and he knew it.

Now it was payback time, he was going to make some serious money. And the consulting side of this accounting firm was his first stop.

He spent the whole interview day there moving up the pecking order. The higher he got, the more time they spent with him. Good sign. They listened to the army problems he'd solved and how he'd done it, even discussing similarities with some of their current industrial clients.

At about 5:45, the consulting division managing partner was all smiles. "Larry, you've had quite a career." And as they walked to the door of his office, "Tell me, any final questions I can answer for you?"

More out of curiosity than anything, Larry asked what performance review process the firm itself used.

"Well, that's easy," the partner said, still smiling. "We have annual reviews for all employees. Everybody gets personal goals set for them, quantified where possible, and they're evaluated against those goals. They're told what their strengths are and what needs improvement."

Larry couldn't help but respond to that, it was his field after all.

"Really? That's surprising, that kind of one-way, top-down evaluation. In business today, it's two-way communication, continuous feedback, questions, coaching. A once-a-year review just isn't enough. I'm surprised you still do that."

The partner kept smiling, but the smile became a little frosty around the edges. "Well, thanks, Larry, I appreciate your opinion. That's *my* system. I'll try to do better next time. Thank you again for coming in."

Two days later Larry got a standard rejection letter.

*Criticize a potential employer at your peril. Somebody is responsible for what you criticize, and you don't know who. It could be your interviewer.*

# Challenge

*I would rather fight with my hands than my tongue.*
Memoirs and Letters of Dolly Madison, 1886

*Youth is not a time of life — it's a state of mind.*
Samuel Ullman, 1934

**B**ernard convinced himself: you've had a long, successful selling career; now it's time to do what you've always wanted — start your own business. And he did, successfully.

But after two years of working seven days a week, he wanted a life again, time to compete in the championship backgammon and bridge tournaments he missed and to play with his new grandchild. It'll be easy enough to get a sales job, he reasoned, and I can live nicely on less money. With my knowledge and experience, any company'll be happy to have me. So, to get his weekends back, he gave up a six-figure income.

The reality was different. Prospective employers looked into his 59-year-old face and found appropriate legal excuses to reject him. The year after he sold his business, he earned $14,000.

Then he got an interview with a financial services firm on Wall Street. The human resources director was 28 and physically small compared to Bernard's 6'2" bulk. For some reason, maybe his lack of experience, he didn't dance around the age issue like the others, but let it be known right away that the company wanted younger, more energetic people in its sales force.

Frustrated and angry, with no recourse open to him, Bernard stood up, leaned over the desk and challenged: "Do you play backgammon?"

The young man pushed his chair away from the desk, out of Bernard's reach, and stammered, "Um, yes, yes, I, uh, play backgammon."

"Good. I'd like to play you for $100 a point, and then I'll wrestle you."

"Uh, wrestle?" the younger man choked, "really wrestle?" He moved further away. "You don't want to do that first?"

"No!" Bernard menaced. "After I get through with you, sonny, you'll be in no shape to play backgammon."

The interview came to an abrupt end.

*Whether you choose to fight age discrimination or forget it,*
*your first priority is to stay focused on finding a job.*

# On Display

*Then the eyes of both were opened,*
*and they knew they were naked.*

Genesis 3

T he economy was bad, so Barry's career counseling business was good. In fact it was booming. Clients flowed into his suburban Charlotte, North Carolina home-office in a steady stream. Many came in the evening, and with a young, exuberant family sharing home and business quarters, he felt perhaps his professionalism was being undercut.

It came to a head one evening during an interview training session with Blanche, an older woman who looked remarkably like Barbara Bush.

"Ignore distractions," he advised her, "stay focused on the interview," all the while talking over his daughter's blaring music video and his three-year-old son Ethan's happy splashing in the bathtub. Blanche listened attentively and ignored the noise around them.

Suddenly the office door flew open and Ethan burst in, dripping wet and totally naked. Giggling wildly, he paraded around the room until Barry's wife, right on Ethan's heels, scooped him up in a big bath towel, the two of them laughing gaily.

Barry was apologizing profusely when Blanche interrupted. "Barry, I raised two kids and have three grandchildren. If this is the worst, you're a lucky man. Now, I think you were talking about ignoring distractions?"

They completed the session with Blanche amused and Barry seriously questioning the cost-benefit of an office at home.

Not long afterward, he moved his business to an office suite ten minutes from home, where he now has a partner and a still thriving résumé preparation and interview training business.

*Distractions will occur at an interview. You can*
*demonstrate your value to an employer if you think*
*on your feet, react appropriately and stay focused.*

# Healthy Glow

*The faces of the soldiers and officers were dark brown:*
*nuclear tan.*

Medvedev, G. "Chernobylskaya Tetrad," 1989, pp. 98-99.
In Z. Medvedev, *The Legacy of Chernobyl,* 1990, p. 168.

"**I**t's only temporary, but it pays well," the employment agency counselor told him.

I'll say it does, Clark thought, a whole lot more than I ever made as an elevator repairman, even after 23 years. "How come? What are they doing, digging gold or something?"

"No, they're cleaning the nuclear power plant reactors. They do it once every 30 years. You'll get full personal protective equipment and a radiation badge. The job lasts three months or until your badge registers maximum exposure, whichever comes first."

It sounded good to Clark. He'd been laid off for eight months now and needed the money. He'd never thought much about radiation one way or the other, but it couldn't be so bad, could it? It sounded safe enough.

Then he met Mr. Stoner. The plant personnel manager looked like a poster boy for some radical antinuclear group. His head was large, out of all proportion to his body, and his face was a reddish color with patches of skin that looked about to fall off. I wonder how many radiation badges he's used up? Clark thought.

At the interview, they never talked about Clark's qualifications or the job itself. Mr. Stoner was more interested in general intelligence. He liked the fact that Clark was used to working alone in confined spaces. They were through in 15 minutes.

The next day, Clark refused the job when it was offered. "Why?" the surprised agency counselor asked. "I thought you wanted that job."

"Well, the money sure was tempting. But I got to thinking, and that guy Stoner, the way he looked. What caused that? And he works in the office, not even in the plant. No, I don't think I want to chance it."

Clark finally did get a job repairing elevators in the Metro, the subway system serving the Washington, D.C. area.

*If hazards are an inherent part of a job,*
*and being a hero is not your style, decline the offer.*

Chapter 6

# Don't Let
## the
# Door Hit You

# No Place Like Home

*He shall return no more to his house,*
*neither shall his place know him any more.*

Job 7:10

Tweeeeet! The final whistle saw the Data Processing Deadheads defeat the Embezzlers from Accounting 21-19 in the South Street Dye Works Six-Person Mixed Volleyball League. Henry, who owned South Street Dye, was the regular referee. He sat down and popped a beer.

Players headed for the showers in the company gym. Spectators departed. And, as usual, a few people from other teams took the court to get in some practice. Nick was among them.

Recently hired, Nick was 50-ish, overweight, uncoordinated, a heavy pipe smoker...and a volleyball freak. He was on the floor every night and always among the last to leave. Watching him, Henry thought: Good for him. That man has true persistence, an athlete's attitude if not his body.

Nick was as good a quality control chemist as he was a terrible volleyball player. In six weeks, he had devised new and more accurate sampling, assay and recording methods that cut rejects by 35 percent. And he always volunteered to do the testing on early morning raw material deliveries. Like every other South Street Dye professional employee, he had his own key to the plant.

Then came the fateful Sunday morning.

Henry, the owner, was an avid golfer. He had a 7:30 tee-time and discovered he'd left his new putter in the office. No problem, he'd pick it up on the way.

He pulled into the back lot at 7:10, and wondered who owned the rusting 17-year-old Sedan de Ville with the cracked windshield and wire hanger for a radio antenna. Probably gave out Friday night and somebody'll pick it up tomorrow, he thought. Anyway, he was in a hurry. He unlocked the door and strode toward his office.

What the hell is that?

Music echoed down the hall. Bob Dylan music. From the technical department.

Henry followed it. There, that office. He pushed the door open, and his jaw dropped like a largemouth bass attacking its dinner.

**166**

There sat Nick. In tan pajamas, threadbare bathrobe and fuzzy slippers. A mug of coffee in one hand, the entertainment section of the *Sunday New York Times* in the other. Mr. Coffee machine and boom-box on the file cabinet, portable TV on one corner of the desk, hot plate on the other, the newspaper scattered in between and blue-gray pipe smoke everywhere. Both Nick's and Henry's eyes bulged.

"What...is this?" Henry stammered.

"Uh...good morning, sir. Actually, you see, um, I've been living here."

"*Living* here!"

"Uh, yes sir. I only meant to do it for a couple of days until I found my own place, but it's really not bad. And I'm saving a fortune."

Henry was fascinated. "And nobody noticed?" He piled the newspaper on the floor and sat on the desk.

"The volleyball league solved everything, sir," Nick explained. "After practice I shower and shave, go out to eat and come back around 10. I set the alarm for 5:30 and get to the lab a half-hour before the early birds."

"Where do you sleep?"

"On the couch in the conference room. It's really pretty comfortable."

"Your clothes?"

"I pick up my suits and shirts from the cleaner as I need them, and use this cardboard box as a dresser." He opened it — socks, underwear and T-shirts neatly folded and stacked.

"How do you get your mail?"

"Post office box, sir. Look, I hope all this isn't a problem, I could pay rent."

It turned out to be a big problem. The lawyers said that Nick's living in his office voided the plant's insurance.

Nick was fired. Plant security was upgraded to an electronic ID system, with a computer to record off-hour entries and exits. All employees surrendered their keys.

But the volleyball league continued. Without Nick.

*The old saying that "Home is where you hang your hat"*
*was never meant to include the office.*

# Waffle

*We know what happens to people who stay
in the middle of the road. They get run over.*

Aneurin Bevan, 1953

"What do you think, Mom, the gold or silver earrings?"

"Honey, they both look good."

"I think I like the silver. But then again, maybe the gold. The tear-drop dangles? Mom, help me."

"Debbie, go to work!"

That was Debbie, a personnel administrator by vocation and habitual vacillator by inclination.

One day at the office, while she was talking to an outside recruiter, he asked if she'd be interested in another job — ten percent more money, right in town, a good company. "That sounds good, Jim," she said. "Yeah, I mean, I guess I should at least talk to them, right?" And they set a date.

When she took the day off and interviewed at the new company, Jim was right — nice offices, the people were friendly and they seemed to like her. But on the other hand, it was a lateral move, new procedures to learn and, well, she just wasn't sure.

A week later Jim called with a firm offer, including the ten percent raise. "Congratulations," he said, "it's a great job for you. When can you start?"

"Gee, Jim, I don't know," Debbie waffled, "really, I don't know what to say."

"Whataya mean you don't know?" he almost shouted. "Debbie, it pays $250 a month more and they loved you. It's a perfect fit. What more's to know? Debbie, don't blow it."

"Yeah, I know, but...well, Jim, I like this job too, the work and the people here. Let me think about it, okay? I'll call you in the morning."

About an hour later, Jim called back. "Debbie! I spoke to them again and they'll go 12 percent. They love ya, babe, but they have to know now, today."

"Jim, I'm just not sure. It's such a big decision."

"Look, Debbie. It'll take two years to get 12 percent where you are now. I guarantee, if you turn this down you'll kick yourself next week."

Debbie hesitated a long moment, hemmed and hawed, back and

forth, and finally said, "Well, okay, Jim, I guess I'd better take it. You're sure it's right? Okay, tell 'em then, but I have to give two weeks' notice."

That afternoon she typed up her resignation and handed it to her boss. He was completely surprised. He thought she was happy in her job. "It's really a bad time, too, Debbie. I have to get those new organization charts out, you know that. I was counting on you."

"Yeah, I know," she murmured, feeling guilty.

Debbie worked extra hours the next two weeks, trying to finish up, but there was no way to complete it all. And on the day before she was to leave, her boss offered her a 15 percent raise if she'd reconsider and stay.

Wow, super! Even more money. The same job, all my friends, nothing new to learn. But...I already told them, they're counting on me. But still.... Finally, she accepted the boss's offer.

"Are you out of your mind?" Jim did shout this time. "You can't do that. You accepted. They turned down two other people, sent out a memo on your appointment. You can't do it, Debbie. How would you feel if *they* changed their minds after *you'd* already quit?"

"I'm sorry, Jim," she said, "I really am, but it's better this way. I think this is what I really want now," and hung up.

She worked hard and got the new organization charts and the department budget completed in the next two months. That was when the boss told her she was laid off, part of an ongoing restructuring, he said.

But Debbie knew the boss didn't trust her anymore. He used her to get through the crunch, and when it was over, he could take his time looking for a replacement. And Jim, the recruiter, wouldn't even take her calls.

*"More than 80% of those accepting counteroffers leave or are terminated within 6 to 12 months."*

Baty, R. Gaines, "Beware of Counteroffers," *National Business Employment Weekly,* April 24-30, 1994.

# Golf Buddies

*Golf is a perfectly good walk — ruined.*

George Bernard Shaw

**B**rian pulled into the golf course parking lot and felt a faint stab of guilt. A month ago, he'd gotten his B.S. in engineering, but after weeks of unsuccessful job hunting he was beginning to worry about his prospects. The self-imposed pressure was mounting.

I need a break, he'd told himself over coffee that morning, I'm getting extremely teed off. Which gave him an idea. He'd been paying his dues, he could afford to take a morning off. Time enough for pavement-pounding later. So he drove to the town golf course for a quick nine holes.

The public course wasn't crowded; most people were working. Brian spied a trio of retirees and asked to join them. "Glad to have you," the pleasant looking chap with clear blue eyes said, "I'm Mike." He introduced the others as Bob and Herb, and they set off for the first tee.

The hole was a soft dogleg to the right. Herb was first up, and Brian found himself standing next to Mike. "So, tell me, Brian, what's a young fellow like yourself doing playing golf this early in the day?"

Brian explained about his job situation. "So this morning, I decided to blow off some steam. But this afternoon it's back to the fray for me."

"Well, you know," Mike said as he pulled the driver from his bag, "my nephew is human resources manager at Boscobel Manufacturing in town. Ever heard of it?"

"Sure, who hasn't?" Brian said. He paused as Mike took his first shot, fading far down the fairway, nearly driving the green. "Nice one! Boscobel, yeah, they're a well-known firm."

"I'll take that one," said Mike enthusiastically, "birdie for sure. Anyway, Brian, I know they're looking for an entry-level engineer. The ad hasn't gone in the paper yet. If you like, I'll give my nephew a call for you."

"Say, that'd be wonderful. I'd appreciate it."

Brian couldn't believe his luck. Even better, Mike actually followed through. The next day, his nephew, Jeffrey, called and they discussed the job — electrical engineering, Brian's major in school — and the following week he went in for an interview.

Jeffrey was only a few years older than Brian. "So you play golf with my Uncle Mike?" he asked, leading the way into his office. "That's great. You know, for a public course, I think this town does a pretty good job with it, don't you?"

**171**

"Oh, do you play?"

Jeffrey laughed. "As much as I can!" He and Brian spent the next half-hour talking about golf, the courses they'd both played, the new types of clubs on the market, a few funny stories traded. Soon Jeffrey's secretary stuck her head in. "Boss, you've got a meeting in three minutes."

As Brian was leaving, Jeffrey shook his hand warmly and said, "We're really going to have to get together and play sometime."

Brian drove home happily. He'd never gotten along so well with anyone in an interview before. Yessir, he said to himself, a new job and a new golf partner. Not a bad day's work!

The next day he waited by the phone, assuming he'd get an offer from Boscobel. But no call came that day or the next or even the next. On the fourth day, Brian received a standard rejection letter, signed by his friend Jeffrey.

Shaken, he just had to call Jeffrey and find out why.

"I'm really sorry, Brian, I think you're a terrific guy, no doubt about that, and you'd really have fit in here well."

"Then what in the world..."

"Well, I just wasn't sure if you were qualified for this kind of work. It requires a pretty solid knowledge of electrical engineering, you know?"

Brian took a deep breath. "Sure, I do know it, Jeffrey," he said. "And I have that knowledge and background. Can I come back and maybe we can discuss it?"

"I really wish you'd mentioned that, Brian. Why didn't you?"

"I, uh, well, I guess we sort of got off the subject," he replied sheepishly, "finding out we had so much in common and all."

"Boy, I am sorry," said Jeffrey, "I really am, but I just didn't know, and we filled the job yesterday."

"Oh."

"But good luck in your search, Brian. And, hey, I'm still looking forward to playing a few rounds with you sometime."

"Actually, Jeffrey, I think I'm going to cut back on golf for a while," Brian replied. "I'm considering racquetball."

◎

*Spend no more than a few minutes on chitchat*
*and then get to the point—ask questions about the position,*
*present your qualifications and when the interviewer talks, listen.*

# Art Lover

*She ransacked her mind, but there was nothing in it.*

Joyce Carol Oates, 1970

*The Metropolitan Museum of Art stands on a 17-
acre complex bordering Central Park on Fifth
Avenue in New York City. It has been called
"...the most diverse and dazzling art museum in
the world and, odds on, the richest in history."*\*

Veronica, an accountant, stood at the curb watching.
Taxis deposited fashionable women in long furs and shiny,
pointed boots. A school bus from New Jersey disgorged a horde
of noisy ninth-graders. New Yorkers, out-of-towners and obviously foreign
visitors speaking odd languages...serious art students, working people
and retired people...male and female, rich and poor, art lovers all, mingled
on the broad sidewalk before ascending the long granite steps under tow-
ering marble columns.

My God, she thought.

Veronica was about to have her third and final interview for a mid-
level accounting position, and she was going to meet the museum's president, too. Understandably, she was nervous as she entered the spacious,
vaulted stone foyer, removed her coat and headed toward the administrative offices. About a half-hour into her interview — she was doing very
well; she was good at her work and knew it — the president joined them
carrying a cup of coffee in a delicate china mug. He was distinguished,
urbane and articulate, as she'd expected, and obviously passionate about
art and the museum. He's great, just great, she thought, as they chatted
cordially about the museum's accounting needs. Then he asked, "Tell me,
Veronica, you know our salary is not what you could earn in the commercial world, what attracts you to us?"

"Well, it's really convenient for me; I live only ten blocks away. I'd
like to see some of the exhibits, too. I haven't been here since my sixth-
grade field trip."

The president's eyes narrowed and his jaw hardened for a long
moment. Convenience was not the answer he expected, or wanted. The

---

\* *Making the Mummies Dance,* Robert Hoving, former director, Metropolitan
Museum of Art.

challenge of the job, yes, association with a world-renowned institution, the famous art and artists, special exhibits, cultural activities, the excitement, the prestige, any or all of these, but not convenience. There was obviously little interest in the arts here.

Veronica noticed the slight frown as the president politely excused himself, but she had no inkling why. The interview concluded soon after, and the next week she was informed that the museum had selected another candidate.

*"Why" questions are important to interviewers.*
*Show your enthusiasm for the job and interest in the company.*

# Crisis Center

*No one can make you feel inferior without your consent.*

Eleanor Roosevelt

With a master's degree and seven years' identical job experience in Alabama, Mary was confident she'd get the crisis hotline director's post in the Tidewater Virginia community where she'd recently moved. The meeting with a panel of six local interviewers convinced her. They left no doubt she was the best qualified.

They even acknowledged it in their letter, the letter saying they'd offered the job to a long-time resident with lesser credentials, but someone they all knew.

It was no consolation that, in the same letter, they asked Mary to *volunteer* her time and expertise! She was more knowledgeable than the new director, they said, and he could use her help.

*When it's obvious you're being squeezed,*
*it's easy to decline the invitation.*

**174**

# Squeeze Play

*Why buy the cow when you can get the milk for free?*

Anonymous

Cosmetics is a risky business. Ask Victoria. She lost a $60,000-a-year-plus-company-car marketing job when sales of several prestige product lines declined.

But not to worry, she thought. A vibrant redhead with personality and confidence to match, she mailed her résumé to all the major cosmetics firms in New York and got an interview only a week later. She'd gone through all the lower echelons, and was now talking with the marketing vice president for the second time, a good time to talk salary.

"With my experience, I should be able to earn at least what I was making before."

"Which was?"

"Sixty thousand."

"I don't see that's a problem," said the VP, to Victoria's relief. "But tell me, if you were in this job now, how would you introduce this new lipstick line I mentioned?"

That was the type of question Vicki could warm up to. With the money thing settled, she relaxed and spent the next 45 minutes explaining all the marketing ideas she'd implement to launch the new line. The VP listened and nodded.

Got 'im, she thought, when he called the next day. But he wanted to talk some more. "You know, Vicki," he said, "I like your ideas. They're good. But they're marketing theory. If you could be more specific, it'd help me decide. Can you come in Thursday afternoon?"

Theory? I'll show 'im. I'll give 'im specifics! And she spent two hours Thursday talking packaging, pricing, distribution, advertising, tie-in programs, holiday promotions and more. She was sure the VP was impressed. He shook her hand warmly and said she'd be hearing soon.

Victoria was invited back the next week — to get the job offer in person, she was sure — but the VP asked what she'd do with the company's moisturizers. Incredibly, she had a total of seven interviews with the same vice president, each time talking about a different product line. Finally, on the seventh trip, he told her he'd definitely make a decision by the end of the week.

Three days later, the Personnel Department called and did, in fact, offer her a job — at a salary of $30,000.

She turned it down. And felt used, ideas squeezed out of her. She considered suing but had no provable case: they did offer her the job at a salary she now suspected was always $30,000.

Faced with closed doors and dead ends, Victoria applied to nursing school and was accepted.

◎

*Follow-up interviews and specific discussions are common, but red flags should be flapping if you meet the same people on repeated visits, are asked to offer solutions to ongoing problems, develop strategies or be innovative. You have the right to say, "Hire me and I'll tell you."*

# Rectory

*Make a joyful noise to the Lord.*

Psalms 100

Two of his biggest clients died and left their money to children who bought houses with it, not stocks and bonds. The market was lousy. Nobody was investing. People had their money in CDs, or in their mattresses. And Donald O'Hearn, investment counselor, was hurting.

When his friend, Harris, suggested, "Why don't you talk to Monsignor Fallon, I hear the church has some money to invest," he was skeptical. Dollar bills from the collection basket wasn't his idea of investing, but Don was ready to try anything. He called.

"Donald! The Lord does work in mysterious ways. I'm glad to hear from you. I do need financial advice, and I'd be happy to hear your ideas. Can you come by the rectory for lunch today?"

Monsignor Fallon, a spry man of 85, answered the door himself and led the way into the dining room. Don was a "Christmas-and-Easter" parishioner, but the rectory was exactly what he expected — neat, spotlessly clean and quiet, as if God wouldn't let a loud noise penetrate.

Lunch was a fine roast beef with salad and vegetables grown by the Monsignor himself in a little kitchen garden. Two young priests and a visiting missionary-priest from Africa ate with them. The quiet conversation ranged from the church's mission to the Pope's latest travels. Money was not discussed.

After lunch, they sat in the Monsignor's office and the money talk began. "As you may know, Donald," he began, "we've been raising funds for a new school wing. This is a wealthy parish, and the people have been generous. But we estimate that construction can't begin for at least two years. In the meantime, we want to invest the money wisely."

"Of course," said Don, nodding sagely. "About how much money has the parish raised so far, Monsignor?"

"Four hundred and fifty thousand dollars. It's in CDs now, earning about three percent. Do you think we could do better?"

Don's mouth watered. The old priest said four hundred and fifty thousand dollars without blinking an eye, as if he were talking about a grocery list or the weather. Three percent? He could do better throwing darts at the stock listings.

"I think I can help you there, Monsignor," replied Don, trying to keep the excitement out of his voice. "Could I see where the funds are now?"

"Father Bob here can help you with that. He keeps track of those things on the computer over there."

"Would you like to take a look, Mr. O'Hearn?" asked the young priest in a soft voice.

"Yes, if I could."

Father Bob booted up the PC and brought the records onto the screen. He then offered the chair to Don, who eagerly sat down and swung his legs under the desk... smashing his kneecap on the point of the metal drawer.

"#@*%#&*}|#*!" Excruciating pain! In a visceral reaction, Don let out a string of obscenities never heard before or since in that quiet rectory.

Five seconds and Don realized what he'd done. The young priests were shocked. The Monsignor stared. The relationship changed.

"Oh, *Lord,* Monsignor," he stammered. "No! No, I mean...uh... that is...look, Monsignor, I'm *very* sorry!"

But the damage was done.

"Well now. You can look at those figures any time, Donald," the Monsignor said in a soothing tone. "Right now, I think it's more important to go home and put some ice on that knee before it swells up. We'll talk again soon."

Father Bob ushered Don out, and he never saw the inside of the rectory again. He called the Monsignor several times, and the old priest was always polite but never again invited him to discuss the church's investments.

*People like to work with people like themselves;*
*"blending in" is important.*

# Jack of All Trades

*No man can be a pure specialist without being,*
*in a strict sense, an idiot.*

George Bernard Shaw

**K**aren, a technical writer, worked as a consultant "to get paid what I'm worth — every project, every time." When a recruiter placed her at a large financial institution to update the user's manual for its computer system — a long-term project right up her alley — she was delighted.

On her first morning, just settled into the pleasant, functional office the company provided, the department head walked in.

"Jack," she greeted him, "nice digs. I'm moved in now and rarin' to go. When can I start?"

"Well, that's what I wanted to talk to you about, Karen. We've got a problem. The programmers hit some snags and the system's not up yet. Go down there and help 'em get the glitches out, will you?"

"Uh-oh. Say, Jack, I'd love to help, really I would, but that's not my field. I don't know anything about programming."

"Hey," he said, "I've got a problem here and I have to get it fixed. You're a consultant, and consultants are supposed to know everything. Help me out, will ya?"

"Jack, I'm a technical writer, not a programmer. Look, if someone paints cars for a living, that doesn't mean he's a mechanic and can fix the engine."

That only made him angry. "Okay, Karen, if that's the way you wanna play it. But know this: I don't like people who play 'that's not my job' games with me!" He stormed out of the office.

Upset, Karen called the recruiter and explained the situation. He came down personally and talked to Jack, who just kept repeating, "Consultants are supposed to know everything and she wouldn't help."

Karen's first day on the assignment was her last.

*Roll with the punches and move on.*

**179**

# Too Comfortable

*It ain't over 'til it's over.*

Lawrence (Yogi) Berra

Central New Jersey, 1991, and times were hard. Craftsmen and laborers in beat up old station wagons pulled into our industrial park almost every week, stopping at every plant and warehouse looking for work. There were no jobs to be had, so they'd move on to the next park.

One Tuesday morning, though, a shiny black Mercedes pulled up and Walter arrived. He was about 60 and wore a dark conservative business suit, but like the others, he visited every plant in the park. When he got to ours, Peter, the plant owner, decided to talk to him, more out of curiosity than anything, I think.

Walter was a production engineer and had been chief operating officer of a company ten-times our size. He'd also been out of work for more than a year. Now he just wanted a job, needed one is probably closer to the truth. "Anything," he said, "anything at all." It must have been a humbling experience.

"I tell you what," he said when Peter hesitated. "Let me look over your shop and make some suggestions. If you like my ideas, hire me. If not, don't, and it costs you nothing."

How could Peter refuse? He agreed to pay a one-day consulting fee and asked Walter to come in the next day.

Walter was there at 7:30, eager and energetic. He talked with Peter for an hour, then to the machine operators, the foremen, the supply room and shipping clerks, the accountant. He diagrammed the work flow and poked through the tool crib. He studied the inventory and purchasing records, everything. We left the plant together about 6:20 that evening, and he was excited.

On Thursday, he and Peter were closeted all morning. When they came out, I overheard Peter saying, "You know, if I can increase my through-put with less inventory like you say...." They walked off into the plant with Walter talking and gesturing and Peter nodding.

They came back at about 3 o'clock. Standing right behind my desk, they shook hands and I heard Peter say, "Walter, I like it. It'll work. Come in tomorrow and we'll go to lunch and talk about a job for you." Good for Walter, I thought. And you, too, Peter.

**180**

Well, Friday morning was not one of Peter's best. A customer canceled a big order, and the shop people presented him with a union organizing petition. When Walter arrived, Peter begged off. "Walter, I just can't make it today. I've got problems I have to deal with. Come back on Monday and we'll talk." And he headed out to the production floor.

If Walter had just left then, he would undoubtedly have gotten a job offer on Monday. But he didn't. He sat down at Marie's desk, made himself at home and picked up the phone. He dialed — eleven digits. And he talked for a half-hour.

That's not right, I thought, but didn't say anything. Peter did when he came back to the office. "Hey, Walter. What are you still doing here? And leave the phone alone, okay?" He picked up some production notes and ducked back into the plant. Walter waved a vague hand in the air and put his feet up on the desk.

Amazingly, he continued to talk. He even dialed two more long-distance numbers, maybe even international. I guess he just didn't understand small-company mentality. At a billion-dollar firm, the telephone is just overhead. At a private company, it's taking money directly out of the owner's pocket.

Peter came in again and stopped dead still when he saw Walter, lounging back, phone at his ear, feet on the desk. Then he lost it, flipped out completely. I never heard anyone shout GET OFF MY PHONE! that loud. Even more amazing, Walter put his hand over the mouthpiece and calmly said, "Just a few more minutes, Peter."

Peter charged the desk, grabbed the phone and ripped the cord out of the wall. He snatched up Walter's briefcase and heaved it through the door, far out into the parking lot. Then, standing trembling over Walter, neck cords vibrating, finger pointing, he screamed: OUT! Walter got up and left.

On Monday morning, Walter actually showed up again. Peter refused even to see him, but Walter continued to call every week for a month. He never did get it. He still expected Peter to apologize and offer him a job.

*"To me, when a person's a stranger, he should act a little strange."*
*Funny Girl*, 1968 film

# Expert Advice

*An expert is one who knows more and more about less and less.*

Nicholas Murray Butler

J anice, a registered nurse for seven years, had finally had it with low pay, long nights on the pediatric ward, scheduled shifts every other weekend, the chaos and heartbreak of her small charges and the unreasoning demands of their frightened parents. There has to be a better way, she thought.

And there it was, a major corporation's ad: medical sales representative, degree and health care experience required, send résumé. She jumped at it.

Putting her résumé together was a chore. But after three hours at the kitchen table with a pot of coffee and a #2 pencil, even she was impressed with her background as she read it over. The only question was what to put down for education. Janice had her R.N. certificate but was a few credits short of the B.S. she expected to complete in January. What's the best way to handle that?

Vicki, she thought, my friend the big-time executive recruiter, she'll know. Besides, I haven't talked to her in ages. She picked up the phone.

After a half-hour's catching up, Janice put her question about the résumé to Vicki. "That's simple," Vicki replied. "Put the degree on your résumé, but don't put down a date. Human resource professionals understand that means you haven't graduated yet."

Problem solved, Janice thought. But when she brought the résumé to a résumé-writing firm for typing, they told her it would be better to say "in progress" or "expected" next to the degree and year. "A lot of older professionals leave the date out purposely to mask their age."

Confused, Janice called Vicki, who again assured her that omitting the date was her best bet. So she had it typed Vicki's way and faxed it to the company. A few days later, she was delighted to be called in for an interview.

Is this what I've been missing? she thought as they talked. Twice the salary? Company car? Nights and weekends all for myself? Doctors who really talk to me like a real person? Wow!

The sales vice president who interviewed her was just as happy. As a nurse, Janice had actually used the medical devices she'd be selling. She knew hospitals. She was intelligent, organized, aggressive but pleasantly so. With some good sales training, she'd be a natural.

Everything clicked. Janice left feeling sure she had the job, and the sales VP called the very next day to offer it to her. She accepted. "Welcome aboard," he said sincerely, "we're glad to have you. You'll get the formal, written offer in a few days."

Three days went by, four, seven, ten and Janice heard nothing. Finally, she called and got the vice president's secretary. "Who? Oh, yes, Janice. Please hold."

Three minutes later, another woman came on the line. "Hello, Miss Foster?" she said coolly. "Yes, I'm the director of personnel, and I'm sorry to tell you that the job offer has been withdrawn."

Janice was stunned. "But, but why? What happened?"

"We always do background checks, Miss Foster, and we were unable to verify your degree."

"But that was a mistake. Wait, I can explain. You don't understand."

"I'm sorry, but the decision is final. And now, if you'll excuse me, I'm late for a meeting. Goodbye, Miss Foster." And she hung up.

Janice cried. The job was gone. They thought she was a liar. And they wouldn't even let her explain.

She wrote to both the sales VP and personnel director explaining the situation and emphasizing that she had no intention of misleading them. The VP called to say he was sorry, her mistake was understandable but there was nothing he could do. He wished her luck.

◎

*Don't BS about your B.S.*
*Education can be verified with a phone call.*

# Metro North

*It was the best of times, it was the worst of times.*

Charles Dickens, *A Tale of Two Cities*

Gina was full of herself. Times were good. She was on the fast track at an old-line Wall Street investment bank with a hefty salary and growing responsibility. And she loved the bank itself, its 100-year-old traditions, quiet trappings of wealth, and the aura of power and influence that permeated the place.

The only downside was the commute. She spent two-and-a-half hours a day traveling: drive to the station, train to the city, subway downtown, walk to the bank; then reverse everything in the evening.

The train ride wasn't bad, though, especially at night. The same bridge game had been going continuously five nights a week for over three years. Gina was a constant kibbitzer, and finally joined the game when one of the players retired. She was at least as good if not better than he was, and soon became "one of the boys" around the horizontal briefcase.

When Gina got her big assignment at the bank — a major corporate spin-off — she couldn't wait to show off at the bridge table. She talked price/earnings and debt-to-equity ratios, book value and inventory turnover, projected revenues and pro-formas. "Shut up and deal the cards, Gina!"

Unfortunately, she wasn't boring everyone. The anonymous "face" across the aisle — the same face that had been in that same seat every night — was a partner in another investment bank. And he was appalled. Such indiscretion with a client's confidential data is a cardinal "no-no."

The next day, a few phone calls led him to the senior partner in Gina's firm and he described the "girl on the train." It didn't take long to identify her, and Gina was fired immediately, with cause, from the bank she loved, effectively blackballing her from all investment banking.

At her exit interview, a personnel assistant suggested, "Gina, have you thought about Wall Street employment recruiting? That takes strong conversational skills. Your mouth would be an asset."

*Loose lips sink ships. Don't torpedo your career by shooting off your mouth, especially in public, about confidential information.*

# Test

*...when the hour of dire need draws nigh, it may find
you not unnerved and untrained to stand the test.*

William James, *Principles of Psychology*

**B**ob was interviewing for an instructor's position at a driving school. The owner, Hans, was in his late 50s, tall, athletic, close-cropped iron-gray hair, thick German accent. In another time, Bob thought, this man wouldn't be teaching driving, he'd be a riding instructor for the Prussian cavalry.

"My instructors pass this test," said Hans. "I designed it myself, yah? The state driving test, hah! It is so easy, it is a joke!"

"You will sit at that table, yah? You have 30 minutes." Hans set a big kitchen timer on the table. Tick, tick, tick, tick, tick. It didn't help.

There were 100 multiple choice questions about driving procedures, regulations and rules of the road. Bob took a deep breath. He licked the pencil once for luck, and, gritting his teeth, started.

He finished just as the timer went off. Boy, I'm glad that's over, he thought, handing Hans the test and sitting back to watch him grade it.

Hans raised his eyebrows. He blinked, once, twice, looked up at Bob, then back to the test paper. He picked up a red felt-tip pen and began circling things. In a few minutes, he was mumbling to himself in German.

Bob fidgeted.

Scraping his chair back, Hans stood up ramrod straight and pointed a quivering finger at Bob. "Ninety-eight," he shouted, "98 of 100 wrong! Mein Gott! And you have a license? I would be afraid to put you in one of my cars! In Germany you would never get a license, never!"

"Well, I, uh, I guess I don't get the job, huh?" Bob stammered. "I guess I'd better be going."

Driving off, he saw Hans in the rearview mirror, staring out the office window. Probably making sure I don't smash up one of his school cars on the way out, he thought.

*Be prepared. Do your homework before the interview.*

# Bad Timing

*Half the promises people say were never kept were never made.*

E.W. Howe

"I probably shouldn't say this now," the vice president told Don after a full-morning interview, "but you're a shoo-in for this position."

And amen to that, Don thought. Let go as redundant after his bank merged, he'd been on the street for five months. This bank was smaller, but the job and title were bigger and so was the salary.

"Look," the VP said, "it's just about noon. Why don't you join me for lunch? We'll celebrate and talk some more about what you'll be doing."

Don accepted gladly. As they were leaving, the phone rang and the VP turned back to answer it.

"Yes, George, how are you?" He listened a moment.

"What?" His face went pale as he listened. Slowly, he put down the phone. "I've been fired," he announced.

Don started to excuse himself to leave, but the VP straightened up, thrust out his jaw and defiantly declared, "Hell no! Let's go to lunch! It's the last expense account I'll turn in, so let's make the best of it."

He took Don to a very expensive restaurant and downed two martinis before ordering. A third came with the oysters, followed by a good cabernet to accompany the filet mignon, and two cognacs to settle the meal. Getting fired didn't curb his appetite or his thirst.

Sipping the last cognac, he said thoughtfully, "Don, come back to the office with me. I work there until the end of the day. I'm going to hire you."

In the office, he spoke to his secretary who soon brought in an "offer of employment" letter. The VP signed it and gave the original to Don. Starting date was the following week.

The next Monday, Don showed up and was immediately ushered into the human resource director's office. "I'm sorry," he said, "but Ken no longer had the authority to make that offer. I didn't even know about it until this morning. We'll reimburse you for your time and expense today, of course, if you'll sign this release."

Don signed and took the small check. He suspected all along the offer wasn't really valid. It was just too good to be true.

*There's no such thing as a sure thing.*

**187**

# Diplomat

*...a date which will live in infamy.*

President Franklin D. Roosevelt, December 8, 1941,
referring to the Japanese attack on Pearl Harbor.

ob hung up the phone, barely able to contain himself. "Miss Sternbach!" he rapped into the intercom. "It's official, I'm going with them to Japan! I need you to do some things for me."

"Yes, sir, Mr. Perry, congratulations," Sylvia Sternbach said with just the right amount of respect in her voice. Her eyes were wide behind the glasses. She was a little afraid of him, he was sure. That was okay. People in the plant universally referred to him as "Sweet Old Bob," or sometimes just the initials.

He didn't mind. He was proud of his reputation as one of the toughest managers in the company — dogged, relentless, never give up. That's the way he was. And it worked for him, didn't it? All the way from hauling his aircraft commander, Major Weintraub, out of their ditched bomber in the Pacific right up to now as production chief of one of the biggest car assembly plants in the country knocking down a big salary.

After the war, Weintraub had been so grateful that he gave Bob a job in the auto plant where he was personnel manager. Bob made foreman in a year and built a reputation as the guy who could nail production quotas no matter what it took. Promotions came regularly.

But times were changing. Savvy people were saying that the U.S. auto industry better face up to the growing competition from Japan. Bob agreed.

"You know, the brass is finally listening to me," he said to Miss Sternbach. "They're sending some senior people over to negotiate joint production for the new line of trucks."

"Yes, sir," she said deferentially.

"Yeah. And I'm included. They *better* have someone along who knows production. Let's see, I'll need traveler's checks, airline tickets … you know the drill. Check with Betty for the travel arrangements."

It was a tremendous career opportunity for Bob, and he knew it. Just going along for the ride would give him visibility at the top with the management, money and law people, and he intended to do more than just ride along. Yessir, he thought, if I don't come out of this with a VP after my name, I'll eat the biggest sedan we make!

The corporation chartered a jet, and all the way over the group reviewed negotiating strategy, legal considerations, exchange rates and currency hedges, local country content, tariffs, letters of credit and other dull things. Bob sat and listened, irritated that he could add nothing to the discussion. The more they talked, the more aggravated he got.

That's not running a car company, he thought grumpily. Running a car company means time on the floor, sleeves rolled up, dirt under your nails, telling the union rep you'll break his nose if he doesn't stop screwing up your production schedule.

**189**

By the time they arrived at Tokyo International, Bob was tired and crabby. A shower at the hotel perked him up a little. He would've liked a nap, but there was no chance for that. The Japanese had a dinner planned in honor of their American visitors.

"Say, Bob," said one of the executives at his dinner table. "You're not eating much."

"I don't much like Japanese food," he said, trying to squeeze a bamboo shoot between his chopsticks. "Too many vegetables." He gave up and sipped at his sake. "This stuff isn't much good, either. Tastes musty."

The executive laughed. "Better take it easy on the sake," he said. "It sneaks up on you."

The evening dragged on. The Japanese CEO, a small, slim man who could have been any age between 40 and 60, visited each American guest, bowing formally and presenting a small gift in the traditional Japanese custom. Everyone seemed to make a speech back to him. Bob just sat at his table without talking, sipping sake and trying to keep his eyes open. Can' even get a decen' cup a coffee in this crummy country, he groused to himself.

Finally the CEO stopped at his table and offered a beautifully framed decorative map of Japan. "Mr. Perry," he said, "may this small token assist you as you...."

Bob focused on the gift. "Zat a *map*?" He laughed. "Hey, Hashimoto-san, I don' need no map!"

The room went silent.

"No sir, no map. Know 'zacly where ev'thin' is in Japan, ev'r city. Dropped *bombs* on 'em! Mos' of 'em, anyway. Hey, speak'n a bombed, got 'ny more a this sake? I'm startin' to like it!"

By breakfast, Bob was dazed but sober...and on a plane back to Detroit.

*If you drink when money, a job, business*
*or your reputation is on the line, take it easy.*

# Moose

*We cut men's throats with whisperings.*

Ben Johnson

The Board of Directors approved Larry's recommendation. "Do it," they told him, "hire a management consultant to plan a rational restructuring and minimize internal, turf-defending politics. Get it done!"

Larry, vice president of finance for a multibillion dollar, multidivision corporation, interviewed a dozen or more candidates to find the strong academic and professional background he wanted, but with toughness and savvy too. The consultant would have to stand up to the division presidents, all line managers who wouldn't take kindly to a theoretician using mathematical models to tell them which people to fire.

Larry found his man in "Moose," real name Michael. Extremely muscular with a massive chest, Moose had been a star football lineman in high school. He had excellent academic credentials, including the U.S. Military Academy at West Point for two years before transferring out because of "all the nonsense" that went on. "But I'm still proud I went there," he declared. He'd worked for ten years at the division level of large manufacturing companies before joining the consulting firm, and took a very practical approach. Instead of theoretical models, he spoke of implementation and the effects of change on the factory floor.

Larry hired him on the spot — smart enough to produce a good, rational plan and tough enough to hold his own with the division presidents.

Moose waded in immediately, and as expected, the division presidents were resentful, but he didn't let their hostility stop him.

When Larry's secretary came back from vacation, he introduced Moose as "a West Pointer just like your husband." Ann was proud of her husband's military career, and carried a West Point sticker on her car and a little American flag on her desk. She was pleased to meet him.

Until the next morning.

"I have to talk to you," she announced to Larry.

"I can't now, I'll be back about eleven, okay?"

Ann spent the morning on the phone, talking softly.

When Larry returned, she marched in behind him and shut the door.

"Get rid of Moose," she said without preamble.

"In God's name why?" he asked. "He's doing the job."

"I told my husband about Moose last night, and he went into a rage. He knew the name all right! Moose didn't 'transfer out' of West Point, he was expelled, one of the cadets thrown out for cheating in that big scandal, the most disgraceful thing that ever happened there. He brought dishonor on the whole institution. Is this the man you're going to trust to say who keeps a job and who gets fired?"

Larry pondered. If that were true and it got out, the division presidents would gobble him and Moose up like hot dogs, destroy the restructuring, his plans.

"Look, Ann, I'd appreciate it if you didn't mention this to anyone until I've discussed it with Moose and the Board of Directors."

"Of course," she said with a little smile.

But it didn't take long to discover the word was out, undoubtedly from Ann. By noon, he had messages from four division presidents to meet about the restructuring.

The chairman of the board called Larry in that afternoon and told him in no uncertain terms to get rid of Moose. "I can't tell our people that three thousand of them are going to be terminated on the recommendation of a known cheater. Integrity is something you have or you don't have. Get rid of him."

Not only was Larry forced to fire Moose, but the whole idea of using an outside consultant was dropped. A committee with representatives from each division negotiated for six months to determine how many cuts would take place in which divisions. In the end, political pull was the deciding factor instead of what would create a stronger, more efficient company. All because one man had cheated years before.

When the final layoff list came out, Ann's name was on it. Larry made sure of it.

*If you have derogatory information about someone else,*
*handle it like nitroglycerin. It can destroy you too.*

# What To Do

*He's as good as his word, and his word is no good.*

Seumas MacManus

hat to do, what to do, what to do! Accept today's job offer from the major law firm? Or wait for the investment bank to make up its mind next month about the bigger, higher paying job?

Henry, a PC support specialist three months out of work, agonized. He called the bank and, mentioning no names, explained his situation. No help. They liked his background but had more people to see, should they remove his name from consideration? No, he told them, to keep his options open.

"A bird in the hand...," Henry finally decided, and took the job with the law firm starting the following week. All the department heads gave him a welcoming lunch.

At the beginning of his second week, however, the investment bank asked to see him again. He made a lunch-hour appointment and stepped across Broad Street in downtown Manhattan to the bank's offices. He didn't mention that he'd taken another job.

A week later, the bank offered him their job and he agonized again. What to do? Three weeks at the law firm, a commitment here, how will it look on my résumé? I can leave it off. Can I get them to bid against each other? No, I might lose both jobs.

He opted for the bank's higher salary and accepted *their* offer, to start the next day.

Henry waited until after hours to catch the law firm's administrative partner alone and explain that he was resigning and why. Unfortunately, the partner had, for once, left on time.

Another quandary! Start there tomorrow, resign here tonight, but nobody to talk to. The glow from the PC monitor caught his eye, and he decided to type his resignation letter on the partner's PC, explaining how important the extra money at the bank would be to his family. The printer was out of paper, and worrying that someone would ask what he was doing in a partner's office at that hour, he just left the letter on the screen where the partner was sure to notice it.

But the partner was out at meetings all the next day, and everybody else just assumed Henry was ill and hadn't called in.

**193**

Only at 7 pm when the partner returned did he find Henry's resignation letter. He was furious. "Didn't have the guts to tell me himself!" the partner raged. "Worked for us for pocket money while he looked for something better!"

He picked up the telephone and dialed the investment bank's managing director...at home, without looking up the number.

"Seymour, how are you? Good. Frances and the boys, too? Wonderful. Look, Seymour, I'm sorry to call you at this hour, but I wanted you to know about one of your new employees...."

Henry was shocked when the bank's personnel director told him the next day that certain cuts had to be made to trim expenses, and he was being laid off. He'd get three weeks severance, of course, even though he'd only been there two days.

Henry learned too late that the bank was the law firm's largest client — for the past 60 years. Ironically, his three-week pay checks from the law firm and the bank arrived in the same mail. After deductions, the net was almost the same.

*Your reputation is one of your most important assets. Protect it at all costs.*

# Squeeze Play II

*There is no such thing as a free lunch.*

Milton Friedman

*But there is free coffee.*

Anonymous economics graduate student

ugust 22nd. Hot, humid, exhaust from the buses so thick I could barely breathe walking across midtown Manhattan to the recruiter's office. But he had a chief financial officer's job to fill.

His office was bustling when I got there. In August yet, vacation time when job placement almost stops, a very good sign. I understood why when I met him. The man was a pro — about 50, easy to talk to, knowledgeable and *very* sharp. The job was perfect, too. And best of all, he was on retainer to fill it, not a competitive assignment. If he recommended me, it was almost certainly mine. And we were getting along very well indeed.

For two hours now, we'd been talking about the company, the job and my background. He was obviously comfortable with me. We were into small talk now.

"So Greg, what've you been doing to make ends meet while you're looking?" he asked.

"Oh, a little consulting for small, local companies," I answered truthfully, "helping them write business plans to get working capital or expansion loans from the banks."

"Really? Say, would you have time to take on a small pet project of mine? I could use that kind of help. We'd pay you, of course."

He was on the board of a non-profit group providing free job services to minority professionals, he told me, and needed a strategic plan to get corporate funding. "If you're interested, write up some ideas about how you'd do it and how long it would take. Then give me a call and we can discuss an appropriate fee."

It seemed like a perfect opportunity to make some extra money and at the same time get on the good side of a man who could help my career.

Over the next few days, I read all the material he gave me and wrote a step-by-step outline of how a strategic plan should be prepared — not the plan itself, but exactly what I'd do to create one. It came to ten typewritten pages.

I sent it to him with a cover letter and called Monday morning to talk about the plan, my fee and an interview date for the CFO job. He was in a meeting. That day and the next and the next, all week, every time I called. "In a meeting."

He never got me an interview for the CFO job. He never hired me to finish the strategic plan. And he certainly never paid me for the work I'd done.

He got a free guide on how to write a strategic plan and, I suspect, wrote it himself and charged the organization a hefty fee. I'm not even sure the CFO job really existed.

*There are companies that conduct interviews to get free consulting.*
*If asked to prepare written materials for a company,*
*discuss terms and follow up with a letter of agreement.*

# Merger

*The only time I opened my mouth was to take my foot out.*

Anonymous

"Wrong, dammit, they're wrong again! And then they blame me because my products are losing sales and share."

Wesley, a product manager at a large packaged foods company in New York City, complained long and loud, always pointing out that the downward trend started long before he took over the product line. He shared his criticism of senior management with everyone who'd listen.

When he found a new, higher paying job at a rival company, he made a point of telling all the vice presidents exactly what they were doing wrong and how relieved he was not to have to deal with them anymore. He chuckled afterwards and felt great about it.

Until the two companies merged six months later! Wesley was still a product manager, the vice presidents were still vice presidents, and now they all worked for the same company again.

The story became famous, and Wesley was certain everyone was laughing at him. Less than two months after the merger, he resigned.

This time Wesley wrote a simple resignation letter and left with no parting shots.

"I just had to get out. No one wanted to be associated with me. I was the company joke. I could have tolerated almost anything but that — being laughed at."

*It's a changing, shrinking world out there; you never know when you might need those bridges you burned behind you.*

Chapter 7

# There's More to Life

# Boston Marathon

*Hell no! We won't go!*
1960s anti-Vietnam War slogan

*One, two, three, four, we won't fight a corporate war.*
1990s anti-Gulf War slogan

*It was 1980 and Lorie was just out of college. This is her story.*

I was 22, exploring the market for electrical engineering positions, excited and a little scared traveling alone for the first time, flying to Boston for an interview north of the city the next morning.

My flight was late. Rain was pouring down. The rented car's windshield wipers didn't work. It took me three laps around the airport service road to find my way back for another car. I got to my motel late (an hour's drive away) and had to wake the couple running it. They had no reservation for me (supposedly made by the company) and no vacancy. The room they finally found me was thirty minutes farther away. I was stressed and knew I had to get up early. I got little sleep.

Then the company. They made optical sensors for bombs and missiles. My interviewer showed me actual Vietnam War footage and laughed all the way through it. I felt like I was in the Twilight Zone or a Woody Allen movie. I went home.

*[Editor's note: Lorie's next interview was with Bell Labs. See "French, German & COBOL," page 107.]*

*Learn something about the company before you go there.*
*Being shocked by what you see or hear is a good indication that you are the wrong candidate for the job.*

# Challenger

*...from this day forward, for better for worse, for richer for poorer....*
Marriage vow

Where were you on January 28, 1986? That was the day the space shuttle Challenger exploded, killing all seven crew members aboard, including Christa McAuliffe, a high school teacher from New Hampshire.

I remember it clearly. I was out of work and panicking — severance gone, debts mounting, jealous of everyone who had a job, dimwits most of them, and I had to find a job quickly, any job.

We were living in central New Jersey, and I was about to drive to northern Massachusetts to interview for a senior financial analyst job I had discussed with the company's personnel director. It was considerably below zero when I pulled out of my driveway at 6 am. The New Jersey Turnpike was covered in salty slush, and trucks changing lanes sprayed it up over everything. The wipers just moved the dirt around, and the washer fluid froze as it hit the windshield. Accidents everywhere. In other words, a very tough drive!

It took me six white-knuckled hours to get to that beautiful rural New England town. The snow was white there. I remember noticing that.

The address turned out to be an old garage converted to offices. The personnel director was wearing jeans, a sweater and fuzzy house slippers, part of their informal atmosphere, she explained. I wished she'd told me earlier before I'd ruined a new pair of shoes.

The president was wearing what I called dressed-up casual — pants, shirt and loafers expensive enough to leave no doubt he was the boss. He explained that the company was a private money managing firm for a wealthy doctor in town. Then he read my résumé, which he obviously hadn't bothered to look at before.

"Your background is financial analysis, and this is a relatively low-level accounting job." He looked at me, puzzled, as if to say, "What the heck are you doing here?" Polite but not about to waste time, he explained that I was over-qualified, the salary wasn't what I was used to, he wouldn't pay for relocation and he could probably get the person he needed locally. "I'm sorry you drove all the way up here, especially in this weather." He shook my hand and the interview was over.

Exactly five minutes! A six-hour drive for a five-minute interview. In

a rage, I stormed out of that garage slamming every door behind me, and fumed the entire four-and-a-half hours home. Idiots! All I could think of was, I could have said....! I should have said....!

When I got back, my wife, a school teacher, was already home. I came in the door still ranting about the stupid people in Massachusetts wasting my entire day and I could have gotten killed in the bargain. I went on for a good 15 minutes, not even noticing how quiet she was or that only one small light was on. Finally I said, "Well, tell me about your day. Let's hear from someone who actually has a job."

She looked up and I could see she'd been crying. Very softly she said, "We closed school early today. The children were all watching the launch on TV. There was a teacher on board. The science classes had little models in the cafeteria. We were going to have a lift-off party. And it blew up. They were all killed."

We ate a silent dinner and watched the news on TV — the huge ball of fire as Challenger exploded, over and over, as if, somehow, it might end differently if they showed it often enough.

The Challenger disaster put my job search in perspective. I was still truly sorry for the astronauts and their families, but I was more relaxed about my own situation than I'd been in weeks.

*Count your blessings occasionally, even when you're job hunting. Everything is relative.*

# Moving Up

*He has every attribute of a dog except loyalty.*

Senator Thomas P. Gore

A t first, waiting in the spacious lobby, Jeffrey wondered what it would be like to work "up here at corporate." After an hour he wondered how many year-old magazines he could read. He wasn't in a pleasant mood when the vice president's secretary finally came down to get him.

The VP's first words didn't help.

"Okay, Vance, where did you screw up?"

"I don't follow you," Jeffrey replied, startled. "I haven't screwed up anything."

The VP poured coffee from a carafe, swung back to Jeffrey and took a long sip, eyes boring in.

"Your division's trying to foist you off on me, Vance. That means you're a screw-up, a troublemaker or both. Which is it?"

The man's serious, Jeffrey thought, controlling his anger because he couldn't afford to make an enemy out of a corporate vice president.

"Neither, sir," he answered evenly. "They recommended me because I've done a good job at division. They think I could do the same for you."

"Even if that's true, Vance, it's a mistake bringing division guys into corporate. You'll always play favorites. Better to hire from outside."

Jeffrey thought that, at least, was a reasonable concern and spent the next ten minutes assuring the VP that he could be totally impartial.

The VP listened in silence.

Then, "Vance, let me lay it out for you. I happen to think the president of your division is a total incompetent and his way of doing things probably rubbed off on you. Now's your chance to be impartial. Tell me about it."

That was it for Jeffrey.

"I'm sorry if you think that, but I don't agree. Our division is the only one that increased sales, profits and return on capital last year. Corporate expense was up fifteen percent, we cut expenses eight percent. That's good management. I'd like this job, it's a promotion for me, but not by stabbing good people in the back."

He walked out and drove back to the division. That night he updated his résumé, sure that he'd blown both jobs. The next day, the division president told him, "Word came down. I'll be losing you at the end of the week."

"That's faster than I expected," Jeffrey said. "What did they tell you?"

"Well, they said they need you on Monday. Congratulations."

Then the president cocked his head and asked, "They also said they interviewed people from every division and you were the only one who passed the test. What test? What did they mean by that, Jeff, do you know?"

*Interviewing for a new job in the same company carries a special danger. Make sure you say positive things about the job you're leaving.*

# High Anxiety

*Only the strong shall survive.*

Robert William Service, *The Law of the Yukon*

aoul was executive managing partner of a U.S.-based consulting firm's operation in Spain when the first approach came through Stefano, an old friend who worked at a major U.S. computer company. They needed a VP Consulting-Europe. Would he be interested? No.

Raoul later called Stefano with a change of heart. Too late, the job was filled, but would Raoul consider running their Latin American operations? Maybe. Can we talk?

A three-way telephone conversation with Stefano and the company's executive VP-Latin America produced an invitation to visit headquarters in the United States. Plan to be here three weeks, they told him, we'll pick up all expenses. It was set.

Raoul's plane arrived safely at Kennedy International, but not his luggage. It was gone, causing immediate confusion and distress. An omen? he wondered. No, he convinced himself, this happens all the time. Buy new clothes, get on with it. Nonetheless, his stress level began to build.

He met first with Stefano — easy, relaxed reminiscing — but Stefano was called away, urgently. Raoul waited three hours alone in the office examining knick-knacks, titles in the bookcases and the window views; then scanning corporate literature on the end tables; then pacing. What's happening? More stress. Chest pains, too.

Finally, Stefano returned. He was visibly shaken, lower lip quivering, chin and shoulders sagging, mumbling to himself in Spanish. He hardly noticed Raoul, saying only, "I feel sick. I'm going home." Muerte, Raoul thought, what's happened to Stefano? More chest pains.

Stefano was fired, Raoul learned the next day. Would you be interested in his job, they asked — $750,000 salary, stock options, million-dollar home? No, Raoul replied, too much risk. I don't need it or the money, and Stefano is my friend. Consider it, they asked, stay a few more days, talk to a few people.

He did and his anxiety level and chest pain increased steadily. One night he went to the hospital emergency room, it was so bad. They wired him up and kept him overnight.

Days later, the company finally said there was no job of *any* kind for him. Thank you for coming, but go back to Spain. He went back to the emergency room.

And, when the company refused to pay his expenses — airfare, replacement clothing, hotel, meals, transportation, hospital, etc. — Raoul had to protest and negotiate. More stress, more pain, a *third* visit to the emergency room.

Ultimately, the company agreed to pay half his expenses. The interview had cost him a friend, a harrowing couple of weeks and almost $15,000 — for nothing.

*If the interview causes undue physical, mental or emotional stress, the job is likely to be a lifestyle mismatch. Walk away.*

# Ceramics Factory

*Ignorance is not innocence but sin.*

Robert Browning

*It is worse still to be ignorant of your ignorance.*

St. Jerome

My God, Richard realized, looking up from his checkbook. After I pay next month's bills, I'm tapped out, totally broke. I've been "on the beach" four months.

He took the next-to-last Coors Light out of the nearly empty refrigerator, opened it and sat down to review the situation.

Okay, Richard Roth, take it step by step. You're 34 years old, a good CPA, good record with good companies. You're legitimately out of work, they eliminated the department. Résumés are out all over New York City without a bite. The headhunters all say the same thing: job market's lousy on the East Coast, lousiest in New York. And there's no more time, you've got to find a job. Compute.

And there it was, inescapable: go west, young man. Working outside of New York City had never crossed his mind until that moment.

Richard subscribed to a private job-listing service, and two weeks later was on a plane to interview at a small ceramics factory in rural Kansas that needed a controller. He rented a car in Kansas City and drove west for two hours. City born and bred, the open spaces amazed him. He could literally see the road running to the horizon.

Mick, a friendly type who owned and managed the place, said they were expanding and had to upgrade their accounting systems. It was time for a CPA to be running things.

After the interview, they toured the factory and Mick explained, "We make small ceramic fittings for industrial use. The car companies are starting to put more ceramics in their engines, and we're hoping our business will really take off."

The heart of the factory, he pointed out in great detail, was a series of special brick ovens in which the ceramics were fired at tremendous temperatures. "Not your basic house bricks in these ovens," he said proudly. Richard nodded approvingly, as he knew he was supposed to.

"Roth, that's a Jewish name isn't it?"

**207**

Richard was a little startled and considered telling him that was an illegal question, but decided not to. The man just seemed curious.

"Yes, it is," he replied.

"Well, you won't find too many Jews around here. In fact, I don't know of any. The reason I ask, though, is you might find it interesting that the bricks in these ovens are the same type the Nazis used in the ovens they burned all those Jews in."

Richard was too stunned to reply. That was the most offensive thing anyone had ever said to him. And worse, Mick was completely *unaware* of what he'd said. *Not an inkling!* He was continuing the tour, jabbering away.

Richard couldn't respond. His mind was back in New York, with old Mr. Epstein in the delicatessen, his sleeves rolled up, the numbers the SS troops had tattooed on his forearm still visible, still readable.

They finished the tour, and Richard left immediately. Mick invited him to lunch but he refused, saying he had to catch an early plane.

A week later, Mick offered Richard the controller's position and he turned it down despite his personal financial crisis.

The last time I saw Richard, he was working for a large investment company in New York City.

*You're not going to want every job you're offered.*
*If it's not right for you, keep looking.*

# Market Research

*Tis my opinion every man cheats in his way,
and he is only honest who is not discovered.*

Susannah Centlivre, 1724

"Whatever it takes, team!" was Lyle's favorite expression at the sales meetings he called frequently. An ex-football player, he was now a super-aggressive sales manager.

Brock was new to the team. He and Jill were working the phones when a rival salesman came in to talk to Lyle about a job.

"Hey, man, good to see you," Lyle welcomed him effusively. "Let's do this over lunch. Leave your briefcase in the closet. Brock and Jill are here, they'll watch it."

The two had no sooner left than Jill had the briefcase on her desk.

"What're you doing?" Brock asked.

"What does it look like I'm doing?" she replied. "I'm gathering competitive marketing information." She gave him a withering look and returned to the case. "He didn't even lock it," she noted. "The fool!"

She carefully removed and photocopied every item in the bag — price lists, product specs, customer list, order forms, even his personal address book, checkbook and bank statement.

Everything was carefully replaced and the briefcase back in the closet when the two men returned. The salesman picked it up and left without the slightest clue what had been done.

Brock was appalled. He told the story to Lyle, who grinned admiringly at Jill and exclaimed, "Good thinking, babe. Let's see what you got."

To Brock, he sneered, "Man, you've got a lot to learn. We're playing hard ball with the big boys. It's pretty sad a woman has to teach you. If you haven't got what it takes to contribute to the team, then maybe you won't be on it very long."

Brock considered his options for a few days, and then quit. He decided he didn't like the kind of person he'd have to become to be part of that team.

*Ethical conflicts are a valid reason to leave or refuse a job.*

# Open Court

*A rebuke goes deeper into a man of understanding
than a hundred blows into a fool.*

Proverbs 17:10

*Now long retired as a County Court Judge, Carmine
Marasco learned a lifelong lesson early in his career. As
a struggling young lawyer in private practice, he very
much wanted to be noticed by a particular firm, hoping
they'd hire him as a senior associate or perhaps even a
junior partner. His day came.*

Carmine had a small insurance claim scheduled immediately before a major case the big firm was to handle in the same court. Carmine's matter would just take minutes, so a partner in the firm would certainly be in the courtroom awaiting his own proceedings.

This is it, Carmine thought. I'll impress him with my crisp courtroom style, engage him in conversation between cases and slip him a résumé during the day. A perfect opportunity.

The day before his big day in court, Carmine was not surprised to be called to a conference in the judge's chambers with Bill, the insurance company's attorney, an experienced lawyer whom he got along with quite well. The claim had already been settled, and the only issue remaining was approval of his legal fee. No matter how small, fees must always be approved by the presiding judge.

The judge, an older man of Italian descent, was a favorite of Carmine's, and he knew the judge liked him because of their common heritage.

"Have a seat," he said with a friendly wave as Carmine arrived in chambers. "Bill and I were talking about your fee for this insurance case tomorrow. What are you planning to charge?"

"Two hundred dollars."

"No, that's way too low," the judge said. "Normal for this sort of thing is $500. So here's what we'll do in court tomorrow.

"I'll ask you how much you plan to charge, and you'll say $1,000. Bill here will object. I'll agree that it's too high and cut you back to $500. Bill looks good to his company, I'm on record for keeping legal fees down —

remember, I'm up for re-election next month — and you get $300 more than you planned. Everybody's happy."

Bill nodded agreement.

Not quite right, Carmine thought. But then again.... I *have* been undercharging. My time *is* valuable. And I *did* put some work into that claim. Maybe it's worth $500. Okay, judge, whatever you say.

The next day, the courtroom was packed for the big case, and sure enough, there was the partner from the large firm waiting patiently in the front row, talking with a reporter from the local paper. The undercurrent of conversation buzzed steadily as housekeeping matters were disposed of.

Finally, Carmine's case was called, and the old judge smiled at him warmly.

"I understand this is an insurance case that's already been settled," he said, "and the only matter remaining is the amount of the plaintiff's attorney's fee to be paid by the insurance company. Is that correct?"

"Correct, Your Honor," said Carmine and Bill together.

"Good," said the judge. "What fee do you propose, Mr. Marasco?"

"One thousand dollars, Your Honor."

"Does the insurance company have any objection to this fee?"

"Yes, Your Honor, wc do," said Bill. "We feel that's substantially too high."

Then Carmine was blindsided. An angry scowl replaced the judge's smile, and he leaned forward to wave his finger menacingly in Carmine's face.

*"I AGREE! A THOUSAND DOLLARS IS EXORBITANT! YOU SHOULD BE ASHAMED OF YOURSELF, MR. MARASCO, ASKING A FEE LIKE THAT FOR A SIMPLE CASE LIKE THIS."*

The judge actually shouted the words at him, bringing a shocked silence to the courtroom as everyone turned to stare at Carmine, including the partner from the major law firm.

The judge continued coldly and deliberately in front of the now silent courtroom. "I'm going to teach you a lesson, young man. I'm cutting your fee in *HALF*...to $500. That's all you deserve. Dismissed."

Slinking back from the bench, Carmine realized the judge had kept the bargain, but with no warning that it included humiliation in open court. He saw the disgusted look on the face of the major firm's partner and thought, I made an impression all right. Gathering his papers, Carmine overheard the partner say to a young assistant, "Wonderful. We use all the pull we have to schedule our case before an easy judge, and this young jerk puts him in a rage right before we go on."

Carmine never got the chance to work for that firm.

*If your gut tells you it's wrong, it probably is.*

# Widow Maker

*God himself could not sink this ship.*

Titanic deckhand, 1912

DIRECTOR of Finance and MIS, major
Chicago law firm, $100K plus bonus.

**R**on wanted that job so bad he could taste it. He could buy that sailboat he always wanted on Lake Michigan and a real honest-to-goodness vacation every summer for the family. And, not least, get out of chemical manufacturing and into a classy, white collar environment. Whatever it takes, he thought on his way to the interview.

When he got there, on the 22nd floor in a posh conference room overlooking the drive and the lake, he was served coffee in a china cup by a truly chic young secretary. Yes!

The administrative partner who joined him got right down to business. "I'll be blunt with you, Ron, this place has major problems. A new computer system last year never worked from Day One. We're suing and installing another system now, but we're still getting garbage, scrambled decisions from courts around the country and we can't even connect with the research databases we subscribe to. And last week, they told me one of my major clients was 90 days overdue on his bill. When I called him, he faxed me a copy of his canceled check. Very embarrassing. If we hire you, your job is to fix things, get this new system working to spec. What do you think, can you handle it?"

"What system are you installing now?" he asked.

"We're going with IBM's latest client-server hardware. The workstations are 486s and the servers are Pentium-based. Microsoft software."

"Uh-huh," Ron said, "I think I know it. How about staff, how many people will I have to work with?"

"Twelve, most of them clerks, and a controller. She's been with us 20 years."

"What about the time frame?"

"I won't kid you, Ron, we need it yesterday. Even the associates are screaming about our non-existent research capacity, and our financial statements are three months late now. The IRS is all over us."

Hmm. Little red flags. How did a firm like this get into such a spot?

"Sounds like you really do have problems. Tell me, is this a new position or did you have somebody before?"

**213**

"Oh we had somebody, two people in fact, and to be honest, we fired them both because they couldn't get it done. By the time the last guy left, the controller wasn't even talking to him. He was a real delegator, she said, always passing off responsibility."

Hmm. *Big* red flags. Waving urgently.

Two people fired. Maybe I'm smarter than they were, thought Ron, but maybe I'm not. The controller is still here, obviously protected, shoveling it off on two bosses even though financial reporting really is her baby. Why not me, too? And the timing, totally off the wall. The system's a mess, I have to fix it, right away, with no cooperation and only I can fail. A real "Widow Maker"!*

The partner sipped his coffee, and asked earnestly, "Well, what do you think, Ron? Is this the kind of challenge you can handle?"

Sailboat, vacations, beautiful offices. Ron sighed. "No sir, I don't think so. But thank you for considering me."

The next day, he got a furious call from the recruiter. "You're out of your head! I'll call and tell them you've reconsidered, you were confused and really do want that job. Or else you'll never hear from me again!" Ron refused, and later heard the job had been filled.

Well, it's a cardinal rule in the recruiting business: don't stay mad if you can make some money. Six months later, Ron got another call from the same guy. The law firm had fired the new man, and he might be able to have them give Ron another look. Ron politely refused and hung up again.

*Job interviewing is a two-way street.*
*Just as the employer evaluates the candidate,*
*the candidate should evaluate the company.*
*If the job isn't right for you, decline the offer.*

---

* "Widow Maker" is an old sailors' term to describe bad-luck ships with too many fatal accidents. Such ships, they believed, were inherently dangerous and always to be avoided.

# Little White Lie

*If it is not seemly, do it not; if it is not true, speak it not.*

Marcus Aurelius, Emperor of Rome

Bitter, that's what Lisa was. The whole accounting department axed. Severance based on seniority, not performance. A couple of *dead-heads* getting more than she was. And only six weeks before her raise was due. She was counting on that raise. Unfair!

But Lisa was lucky, too. Just three weeks later, she was completing an interview at another big company, and it was looking good.

"Lisa, you'll be hearing from us soon," the human resources director encouraged. "And, look, you never filled out our employment application. Would you take a minute and do it now? Just give it to the receptionist when you leave."

A pain in the neck, she thought, but did it reluctantly.

At the "last salary" question, she paused. Hmm. There's no way they're going to offer more than I was getting before. Six more weeks and I could have said $37,000. Now I have to put down 34. That's unfair. But if I say 37, what I would have been making, I'll come out even. She wrote in $37,000.

The next week, the company had her back to meet the vice president of finance, who liked her background, and then she met again with the human resources director.

"Terrific," he said. "Informally, you've got it, but the written offer won't come for about a week. That's what it takes to check your references, education, prior employment, salary history, that sort of thing."

Lisa felt great, up until that last part.

"Uh, salary history? That might be a little difficult. You see, the payroll people got laid off along with the accounting group," she lied.

"No problem," said the HR director. "Just make a copy of your last pay stub. We can use that."

Panic. The stub would show that she'd inflated her salary by $3,000.

"You know, I included my annual bonus on the application," Lisa dodged. "That comes out separately. It won't be on my pay stub."

"A bonus in general accounting? Unusual, you're lucky," he said. "Well, just bring in that stub too. Or even a copy of last year's tax return. That's okay if you don't have the stubs."

**215**

Getting in deeper, Lisa continued to lie. "The bonus was in cash. I didn't declare it on my taxes."

"A Fortune 500 company paying bonuses in cash?" he questioned. "That's the first I ever heard of that," and the skepticism in his voice said it all.

He did check her ending salary, and a week later Lisa got a formal rejection letter.

*Don't fool with facts, especially routine facts that an employer can verify.*
*On an application, you can leave the "last salary" box blank.*
*If they ask, explain.*

# Stony Reception

*Rescue those who are being taken away to death.*
Psalms 24

The company produced precast panels of marble fused to concrete, giant 80-by-20-foot slabs, 18-inches thick, destined to become the walls of commercial buildings, and Bill was about to become its new operations manager. It was all but agreed. "Come on, I'll show you the plant," the manager he was replacing beamed.

They walked onto the noisy production floor and four of those huge panels were creeping across the ceiling directly above the workers, swaying gently on overhead conveyors, only a ruptured chain-link away from disaster.

"My God!" Bill whispered. "How do you sleep at night?" He backed out the door and quickly put the job and the plant behind him.

*Stark terror over your safety is a good reason to refuse a job offer.*

**216**

# Quota

*It is best to employ honest men,*
*even though they may not be the cleverest.*

Ekken Kaibara (1630-1714)

Good company, good job, good people, Doug enthused on his way back to the human resources director's office after a full day of interviewing.

When he arrived, the manufacturing vice president was there, too, both men smiling and expansive. Encouraging!

"Have a seat, Doug," the VP welcomed him. "I have to tell you, you really impressed my engineering managers. They all had very good things to say. I'd like to offer you the job."

"Wonderful. I'd like to accept it."

"There's just one little problem," added the HR director.

Uh-oh, thought Doug. Why is there always just one little problem?

"We've been under a lot of pressure from headquarters lately to increase minority hiring," the HR director continued.

"Extreme pressure," the VP agreed.

"I can understand that, I guess, but how does it affect me?" Doug asked.

"We need you to do a small favor," the HR man said. "We'd like you to certify on your employment application that you're African-American."

Doug laughed nervously, running his fingers through his long blond hair. A joke? No, they weren't even grinning. He shifted in his seat.

"You're serious?" he asked.

"I'm sorry, but yes, we're serious," the VP said. "That's the way it has to be."

Doug considered the implications and his options and answered, "Gentlemen, I wish you luck. I hope for your sake that Louis Farrakhan's people don't hear about this." And he left.

*Some companies have creative ways to circumvent EEOC guidelines.*
*If such actions conflict with your views, decline the offer.*

# Big Three

*If you pick up a starving dog and make him prosperous, he won't bite you. That's the principal difference between a dog and a man.*

Mark Twain, 1894

kay, let's get this over with, I thought, doodling impatiently as the other MBA candidates straggled into the lecture hall. This is like freshman orientation all over again.

The dean finally stepped to the lectern and began, "Ladies, gentlemen, thank you for coming. *(Yeah, like we had a choice.)* I have one purpose today: I want to tell you a story. *(God!)*

"Once upon a time, we had an MBA candidate very much like all of you — exceptionally good grades, extremely intelligent, personable, sophisticated, confident, assured. This candidate, I'll call him John, interviewed with 14 companies here on campus and got call-backs from every one, including Ford, GM and Chrysler — the Big Three. *(Attaboy, John.)*

"Well, John also thought he was very shrewd. In those days before airline deregulation, a round-trip seat between New York and Detroit cost about $300 coach, no matter what airline you flew, how far ahead you booked it or what time of day you traveled — the same $300.

"So John scheduled his three interviews in Detroit all on the same day and charged each company for the airfare. Nine hundred dollars reimbursed, $300 expense, $600 ahead. And congratulated himself. That's what MBAs do, make money. *(There's a BUT.... Right?)*

"But.... Detroit and the car companies are a close knit community. People move from company to company. Almost everybody in one company has friends or relatives at another. They get together socially. They talk. *(Right. Here it comes.)*

"And so they did.

"At a house party in Ypsilanti the weekend after John was there, someone mentioned how hard it was to attract qualified, eager young people to Detroit these days.

"'Bob,' laughed a GM man, 'look who you work for! We don't have any trouble like that. Just Thursday, in fact, I talked to a terrific young man....' and he described John in glowing detail. 'Thursday?' said the man from Ford. 'I talked to somebody exactly like that on Thursday. Interested in him, too. Hmm. What school did you say?'

"Well, on Monday morning, GM and Ford confirmed it was John. On

Monday afternoon, they discovered he'd been at Chrysler too. And on Tuesday morning, they found he'd left travel vouchers with all three companies. And now, ladies and gentlemen, the moral of my story. John got no offers from the car companies. He paid back the excess travel money. He lost all campus interview privileges. And the incident went into his school record."

With that, the dean stopped. Very slowly and deliberately he scanned the room, made eye contact with each of us.

"That, ladies and gentlemen, is the story I wanted to tell you today. Take it to heart. Dismissed." And everyone but me filed out subdued. *(Whoa, small time, John. You had those car companies ready to bid for you, an auction, thousands, and you blew it for 600 bucks!)*

*Within an industry, there is usually a strong grapevine, particularly in the same city. Assume your interviewers talk to each other.*

*Don't jeopardize an opportunity by being greedy for a few dollars.*

# Pride of the South

*Ain't it just like a friend of mine, to hit me from behind.*

James Taylor, "Carolina On My Mind"

I t was 1975 when J.R. called about an ad for a purchasing agent with a small auto parts company in Brooklyn. He was sure he'd hit the mother lode.

Bob, the company owner, was from Asheville, North Carolina, and J.R., just out of college in New York City, was from Fayetteville. They talked on the phone for 40 minutes.

Finally, Bob pleaded, "J.R., I've got work to do. You come on in tomorrow, hear, and we'll iron out salary, vacation, that sort of thing."

J.R. walked into the office the next morning and introduced himself.

Bob stood and stammered. "Uh, yeah...well, come on in, J.R., I sure am pleased to meet you."

Telling the story for this book, J.R. still shook his head sadly.

"The surprise, the hesitation said it all. He didn't realize I was black. We had the same accent, went to the same shoreline on vacations, rooted for the same teams. It didn't matter. All he saw was my black skin. Two days later I got a rejection form letter."

*[Author's Note: J.R. is now purchasing vice president for a major automotive parts importer and negotiates multimillion dollar purchases from China and Korea.]*

*Employment discrimination based on race, color, religion, sex, age or national origin is prohibited by Title VII of the Civil Rights Act of 1964.*

# Three Months

*No one can earn a million dollars honestly.*
William Jennings Bryan, 1896

*Ah, consulting: last resort for many a job-hunter and Shangri-La for the unhappily employed. Work for yourself and get paid what you're worth; no boss, no politics, no interference. Ahhh.*

For the first time in seven years, Dave was really happy in his work, happier than he'd ever been in Advanced Network Development for the computer company. He was frustrated there, buried in budgets and compromises and short-term decisions that never recognized the technological and commercial potentials he saw.

The best thing that ever happened to me, Dave thought now about the R&D downsizing that had cost him his job. Now he was a legitimately independent consultant and good at it.

After six months of job-hunting without a nibble, a friend steered him to a big cable company's network development director. In the past year, Dave and another consultant, Andy, had developed a broadband ATM switching and transmission system.

We did it, he smiled with satisfaction, and today the director wants to talk to me about preliminary designs for fiber optic/coaxial cable interfaces, control electronics and all.

In the director's office, Dave sprawled comfortably at the small table. "Great job on the ATM system," the director congratulated him. "Took a little more time than I thought, but worth it. Now the next step," and he brought a thick sheaf of notes and rough-sketch diagrams over to the table.

They talked for more than an hour as the director laid out his ideas and Dave asked questions. "Now the key questions for you, Dave: How long and how much? Give me a ballpark."

"Wow," Dave said as he sat back and scratched his head. "That's a bell-ringer. You know, I'd really have to figure it all out, break it down into specifics and estimate time and expenses for each one. And even that'd be a best-case scenario. Can I get back to you in a few days on that?"

"Dave, I need at least a ballpark now. I have to present this at a meeting this afternoon, and I need numbers. I can make a pretty good guess what it'll take, but I have to be sure we're on the same page."

"Well, if you really need it, I'll try. But give me an hour, okay?"

"Sure, stay right here. I want to go down to the labs anyway." The director left, and Dave divided a piece of pad paper into three columns — "Task," "Time" and "Expenses" — and began to write.

An hour later, the director returned. "Okay, Dave, what've you got?"

"Realize now, this is strictly ballpark, don't hold me to it, but bottom-line...eight months and $100,000."

"What? You're kidding me! Come on, Dave, this is a three-month project, 25 grand. What're you using, solid gold cable and connectors?"

"No, really, look, when you break it all down and lay out a realistic timetable like I've done here, it does, it adds up to...."

"No way," the director interrupted emphatically, "no sir. I'm sorry, Dave, but that's way out of line. I'll have to make other arrangements." And the director ended the interview.

In the cafeteria at lunch, Dave saw Andy, the other consultant on the current project, and the director with the same sheaf of notes and diagrams spread over a table off in the corner. They joshed back and forth for about 20 minutes before the director gathered up the papers and left smiling. Andy wore a cat-and-canary grin as he strolled over to Dave's table. "I just got myself a new assignment," he gloated.

"Really? What kind of estimate did you give him?"

"Oh, strictly ballpark and don't-hold-me-to-it, you understand, but about three months and $25,000," he replied with a straight face.

"Come on, Andy, you *know* that's not right, it'll take a lot more than that, a lot more."

"Sure it will, but that's what he wanted to hear, he told me so. And after three months, they'll have so much invested they'll have to see it through. It's business, Dave, business," he said, tapping his forefinger to his temple.

Dave found other clients and never did any more consulting work for the cable company. But his friend there kept him posted. It took Andy nine months to finish the assignment, and when it was over, they kept him busy for two years after that.

*Stick to your ethical guns. Honesty may not be*
*profitable short-term, but it's the best policy long-term.*

# Donation

*It is more blessed to give than to receive.*

Acts 20:35

"Do you think I have a chance, Dr. O'Neil? Really? For Chief Resident?" My father, Dr. Jack Farrell, asked those questions years ago when he was doing his residency at a major hospital.

"Ah, that ya do, m' boy, ya do," replied his mentor emphatically. "And I'm goin' ta nominate ya."

Dr. O'Neil was an older man, one of the hospital's more influential physicians and, like Jack, an Irish-American, but much closer to The Old Sod. He knew exactly what county all "his people" were from and was disappointed that Jack didn't.

The Chief Resident's title carried only honor, no additional stipend. But it was a significant honor. All the senior physicians voted, and any one of them could blackball a candidate. In effect, whoever they named was considered by the most experienced doctors to be the best resident physician in the hospital.

A week before the vote, Dr. O'Neil and Jack were having lunch in the hospital cafeteria, and the older man said casually to his protégé, "And by th' way, Jack, I've been asked to take up a little collection for the cause. How much can I put ya down for?"

"You mean the hospital building fund?" asked Jack. "I thought that wasn't until next month."

"No, lad, *the cause,* the *boys,* Jack."

"I'm sorry, Dr. O'Neil, what cause, what boys?"

A little disturbed at the young man's denseness, Dr. O'Neil leaned forward and whispered conspiratorially, "The IRA, Jack, the Irish Republican Army. How much can I put ya down for?"

Jack drained his coffee, then said evenly, "Nothing, Dr. O'Neil. I didn't become a doctor to kill people."

The older man recoiled as if slapped. "I can see I've misjudged ya, Jack, I have." He stalked away from the table.

I hope so, Jack muttered to himself.

Jack didn't get the chief residency. Rumor said a senior physician had blackballed him, but he never found out. When he and Dr. O'Neil passed in the corridors, however, they never spoke to each other again.

Dr. Farrell went on to a long and successful career in medicine, eventually becoming Chief of Obstetrics and Gynecology at Stamford Hospital in Connecticut.

*A superior's request for you to join a club, play a sport or give a donation can be a critical incident in your career. Don't take this request lightly. If you choose to decline, be diplomatic.*

# General's Staff

*We won't be home till it's over, over there.*

Over There, patriotic American song from World War I

In World War I, my grandfather, Raymond Farrell, a young captain in the American army, had been through a great deal of heavy combat. He was ordered from the front line to headquarters concerning a vacant position on the general's staff.

Raymond walked into a different world at the commandeered chateau 20 miles behind the lines. Used to the trenches and the mud, field rations and constant danger, he was awed to see white-jacketed waiters clearing luncheon dishes from linen-covered tables. A group of young officers — the general's staff — in crisp, spotless uniforms sipped coffee from china cups.

"Glad to see you, Captain Farrell," the colonel who was to interview him said in a strong southern accent. "Please join us for coffee."

Ignoring the group's distasteful looks at his muddy field uniform, he sat at the colonel's table and left stains on the cloth. A waiter immediately served him coffee and a plate of small cakes. After field rations, the coffee tasted like nectar and the cakes were exquisite. He ate two, but would have wolfed down the entire plateful if the others weren't there.

"Captain," the colonel began, "we've decided to fill this staff vacancy with a line officer. Your basic responsibility would be to maintain the daily map updates. You'd be billeted here at headquarters, of course."

He led the way into the map room. On the wall were huge maps of the entire front. Little multicolored pins represented the opposing forces.

"As the situation changes, you will update the pins on these maps to show current dispositions," the colonel explained. "Nothing to it, really."

"We'll be interviewing other officers for the job, but the general is impressed with your Yale education and your service record. I think I can safely say the position is yours."

"I'm sorry, sir, but I can't accept it," Raymond said.

"Excuse me?" the startled colonel barked.

"Sir, I can't sleep in a chateau every night knowing my men are dying just 20 miles away. They're men, not pins. When they leave the line I'll leave, but not before."

The colonel appraised him for a long moment with flinty eyes, and Raymond waited for the reprimand.

**225**

Instead, the colonel came to full attention and saluted, saying quietly, "Good luck, captain." He turned and left.

Raymond headed back to the front line. Leaving the chateau, he stole a linen napkin in the now empty dining room, filled it with the remaining cakes and stuffed it inside his muddy uniform.

Raymond survived the war but went through several gas attacks, suffering a collapsed lung. The doctors were sure he wouldn't live long, but he was tougher than they thought. He lived to be 82.

*Do what's right for you.*

# Payback Time

*Never hit a man when he's down. Kick him, it's easier.*

Old Irish expression

Fredda was an early customer, and a desperate one, bursting into Elizabeth's new résumé service one early afternoon almost begging for help.

"Look at this job application!" she moaned, waving a multipage form. "And that's not all. They want a ten-page essay to go with it! They told me to write what I know about the chain grocery business and why I want to work in the industry. Can you help me? Please?"

"Well, it's not a résumé, strictly, but I guess it's like one. When do you need it?"

"Tomorrow!"

They set to work immediately, Elizabeth asking questions and Fredda answering them. At 5 o'clock, for better or worse, Elizabeth ended the interview. She had to start writing. It was well past midnight before she finished.

Fredda reappeared at 9 and whistled when she finished reading it. "Wonderful! How did you do that?"

A few minor corrections and Fredda took the final printout, wrote out her check for Elizabeth's fee and, after many thanks, left happily.

A week later the check bounced. Elizabeth called the bank and found the account had been closed four months earlier, long before Fredda wrote the check. She called Fredda's number, and it was disconnected. She went to Fredda's apartment. Moved. Fredda had stiffed her, deliberately, and obviously added her new address and phone number after the application and essay were done.

Angry, but with little else to do, Elizabeth wrote to the company Fredda was applying to and asked either for Fredda's phone number or if they'd ask her to contact Elizabeth.

"Why?" the company's employment manager wanted to know when he called Elizabeth. She told him the whole story, and he said he'd get back to her.

Ten days later, he called Elizabeth again. "Did Fredda make good on her debt?"

"No, I haven't heard from her," Elizabeth replied. "Do you know how I can reach her?"

"Well, we were about to offer her a job when your letter arrived. I told her about it and my talking to you, and she said she'd accidentally used the wrong checkbook. I asked her to get in touch with you and clear it up. If she hasn't, I don't want her working for us."

Elizabeth never did collect her fee. She chalked it off to experience.

*Don't make enemies out of employment professionals,*
*especially when you're job hunting.*

*Maintain good relationships and build a network.*

# At First Sight

*Any man worthy of the name is willing to make
a fool of himself for the sake of a woman.*

Frank Richardson

Frank thrust his jaw within six inches of the company president and spoke with quiet intensity: "If you ever again refer to her as 'some broad,' I'll break your face."

It was in character. Very early in life, Frank learned how to take care of himself. He grew up in a tough neighborhood of Brooklyn, New York, standing up to the bigger kids on the block. He earned a scholarship to college, studied engineering and graduated just as the Korean War was starting. He got into Air Force Officers Training and became a fighter pilot.

When he left the service, his engineering degree and service record got him a job with a defense contractor on Long Island. He married a girl from his old neighborhood, and they had a son. Life was good.

Then, with their little boy just two years old, his wife was diagnosed with cancer. She died within months, and Frank was alone with a son to raise. He always credited his combat experience with getting him through those times. In war, you learn quickly that life is not fair and feeling sorry for yourself does no good.

He did well with his career and his son. He worked at the Long Island defense contractor for ten years, and then became chief engineer for a California defense contractor, reporting directly to the company's president. He and his twelve-year-old boy moved west. The transition went smoothly.

Two weeks into the new job, Frank walked into the president's suite to drop off a report and pulled up short at the door. There at the secretary's desk sat a truly stunning woman smiling up at him. She was beautiful, classic. Their eyes held, and for a long moment the world stopped.

The president broke the spell as he came out of his office. "Oh, Frank. Good, you have the report. Say, I don't think you've met Anna, my secretary. She's been on vacation since you started. Anna, this is Frank, our new chief engineer."

"Uh, hi, Anna," he stammered, "happy to meet you."

"Nice to meet you too, Frank," she replied in a friendly, pleasing voice and a full smile. "Welcome aboard." She extended her hand and Frank took it. A small tingle coursed down his spine.

"Come on in, Frank, and let's talk about these numbers," said the president.

At lunch that day with the head of his development section, he asked about Anna. "Forget it, Frank," he was told with a short laugh that was almost a snort. "The old man doesn't allow fraternization between the hired help. He lectures on it twice a year. If he even thinks anything's going on, he fires people."

But Frank was not the kind to be scared off. Whenever the president was away, he made up reasons to go in and talk with Anna. Eventually, he asked her out for dinner and she accepted, readily.

Within a month, they were seeing each other regularly. He brought Anna home to meet his son. He talked about his life and his dreams, about his worries as a parent, how hard things had been since his wife died, and Anna listened. She was a wonderful listener.

Sipping a brandy after dinner one evening Frank told her, "Anna, I think I'm in love. Could someone like you feel anything like that for someone like me?"

She laughed gently and took his hand. "Frank, don't you know? You're the first man who ever treated me this way, as a real person, not just a pretty face. You talk, you share. Don't you realize that I love you, too?"

The next week, the president called Frank into his office. Assuming it was about the new program they were bidding, he brought all the data he'd worked up so far. He was disappointed that Anna wasn't at her desk, and surprised to see the personnel director.

"I can come back if you have another meeting," he said.

"No, come in, Frank, sit down. I asked Jeff to join us."

Frank sat, but the president paced back and forth. "I'll get right to the point, Frank. This company has a very clear policy against employee fraternization. It's obvious that you and Anna are seeing each other. I want it to stop."

Frank was stunned. "I don't really see how that's any of your business," he said.

Jeff jumped in. "Oh, but it is, Frank. The rules are clear and specific. They're spelled out in the employee handbook."

"Look, Frank," the president continued in a milder tone. "Nobody likes having to do this, but in the long run it's better for the company. You have a good career ahead of you here if you cooperate. If not, then we'd have to terminate you and even take back the relocation money we paid. You have a boy to take care of, think of him. You don't want to be stuck out here on the West Coast with no job, no money, and certainly no references, all because of some broad."

Frank rose and stepped directly in front of the president, a much taller and heavier man, to make him stop pacing. With no more than six inches separating them, he said, "I've seen my wife die of cancer and I've been in combat. If you think losing a job frightens me, you don't know me. I'll clear out my desk immediately. And for your information, I plan to marry Anna. If you ever again refer to her as 'some broad,' I'll break your face."

The president stepped back, genuinely frightened. There was an intensity to Frank that he'd never seen before in anyone else.

Frank left the company that day. He no longer wanted to work for a man he couldn't respect. He wasn't sure if they could or would have fired him, but they never tried to get the relocation money back.

Anna left the company, too, and they were married less than a month later. Despite the president's threats, Frank got a job with another aerospace company in California and did well in his career. Eventually they moved back to the East Coast where Frank became president of a large defense contractor.

I first met Frank shortly before his retirement. When he laughingly told me this story at his retirement dinner, I asked if he really would have rearranged the president's face. "In a second," he replied without hesitation. The look that came into his eyes even then, years after the fact, told me he was serious. Frank and Anna have been married for 23 years.

*It's only a job, not your life.*
*You can walk away from an untenable situation.*

# Not at First Sight

*... college-educated women who are still single at the age of 35
have only a 5 percent chance of ever getting married....
Forty-year-olds ... have a miniscule 2.6%
probability of tying the knot.*

"Too Late for Prince Charming,"
*Newsweek*, June 2, 1986, pp. 54-55.

"Nope, $40 an hour, nothing less," Linda said calmly, refusing to budge. She found it easy, very easy, to haggle with the New Jersey recruiter because she really didn't care very much what happened. She could afford to tough it out: a 40-year-old, single (again) Ph.D.; top-notch consulting reputation in graphic communications, technical and résumé writing; and a possible assignment waiting for her on Wall Street. It was also five days before Christmas 1986 and she had better things to do, like install software on her new Macintosh.

"Linda," the recruiter got back to her, "they want to talk to you. They agreed to your rate for two technical manuals. Are you interested?"

"OK, why not?"

"Good. I'll meet you in front of their place at 1:30. It should take you about 45 minutes to get there. Here are the directions."

Linda left home promptly at 12:45, but the directions were wrong. After much backtracking and stops at three different gas stations for better directions, Linda arrived 45 minutes late. The recruiter was angry. Linda was livid, first because of the poor travel directions and then the recruiter's high pressure insistence that she had to accept the offer if the company made one. Not a good way to go into an interview.

She started with Jim, the project technical director, who worked in a little cubicle overflowing with PCs and peripherals. He was amiable, walking her through all the details of the system to be documented.

"Look, Jim, I appreciate your willingness to show me the system, but could you skip the details and step through the screens quickly so I can count them. That's how I size the job." Jim was put off by Linda's abruptness and gave her a mental "thumbs down" on the personality interview.

Next, Linda talked with Russ, the vice president of MIS, and he was impressed with her Ph.D., her knowledge, her no-nonsense attitude and most of all, with her *availability*. He was seriously under the gun to meet

**232**

the software shipping date, and he couldn't do it without user manuals. That interview went very smoothly.

"Well, Jim," Russ asked later that afternoon, "what do you think of Linda?"

"Don't hire her. She'll steam roll right over the programmers and they'll never accept her. *And* she works on a Mac. She'll *never* fit in."

For the first time, Russ overruled his technical director and did offer the project to Linda. He had to get the software out.

Linda's Wall Street prospect evaporated and this was now the only game in town. She accepted the offer. After all, she thought, it's only a consulting assignment, not a lifetime commitment.

Linda wound up writing eight manuals for Russ's group that year. She also played poker with the technical staff on Friday nights and went to outdoor concerts with the company brass that spring.

Even Jim changed his mind. Five days before Christmas 1987, exactly a year to the day after their initial interview, Linda and Jim were married. Russ was the best man.

*[Author's Note: I met Linda seven years later when I went to her home-office to have my résumé revised. They had a mixed marriage: Jim's PC upstairs cable-linked to Linda's Macintosh downstairs.]*

*Before you leave for your interview, verify the directions.*
*Then, approach every interview as if it's the most*
*important meeting of your life. You never know.*

# The Coin

*When crew and captain understand each other to the core,*
*It takes a gale and more than a gale to put their ship ashore.*

Robert Browning

I t was March 1931, and my grandfather, Frank White, had an interview — in Costa Rica.

Frank was an engineer for a large, New York-based construction company that installed generating plants and power lines around the world. The company had just won a contract to electrify a remote region of Costa Rica, but they had a problem. By terms of the agreement, the project manager had to be approved by the region's five local mayors, and all six Spanish-speaking engineers the company sent had been rejected. They "just don't understand the people," the mayors complained.

In an effort to salvage the contract, the company sent my grandfather — young and without a word of Spanish, but capable and personable.

Travel in 1931 was not what it is today, and it took Frank four hard days to reach the small town in central Costa Rica. He arrived on a Saturday. On Sunday morning, like good Roman Catholics the world over, he went to church.

It was actually a small cathedral serving the entire region. At least a thousand people, mostly small farmers and Indians from the mountains, attended mass that morning, and the tall, fair "gringo" kneeling in the middle of the church drew more than a little attention. He was comfortable as he chanted the familiar responses in Latin, the universal language of the church. His voice carried.

The discomfort, or at least the confusion, came when the collection basket was passed around.

Clink, clink, clink, clink. Pennies. Everyone was putting one penny in the basket. And Frank suddenly realized the great gap between New York and Costa Rican standards of living. To many of these people, a penny was more of their income than a $10 bill to the average American.

As the basket approached, Frank's confusion set in. How much to give? Obviously wealthier than these people, a penny from him would be insulting. But American paper money would be flashy, ostentatious.

When he had to give something, he put his hand in his pocket and felt the answer — a silver dollar. The basket arrived filled high with pennies, and Frank dropped the large coin on top.

**235**

It hit with a loud, resonant sound that rang out clearly, and the reverberations as it settled into the basket pulsated through the church. Definitely not the sound of a penny. Everyone turned to look at the generous

gringo. Even the priest at the altar turned and, looking directly at him, gave the ritual blessing. Frank bowed his head and prayed.

The next day at his interview, he introduced himself — in English — to the five mayors. "Everyone in the region knows who you are, Señor White," replied the oldest in a very halting voice, but also in English. "We have decided. You will run this project."

"But I don't know Spanish," said Frank.

"Ah, but you know the people, señor. Six other men your company has sent to us, and not one visited the church or gave his respects to our priest. You are the man we want."

My grandfather spent almost eight months in Costa Rica on that project. He learned the language and got to know the people and the country.

"Sí," he used to sigh nostalgically, "uno de los más feliz períodos en mi vida!" — one of the happiest times of my life.

*Going to a new company, across town or across the globe, find out about dress codes and customs. And, yes, sometimes you get lucky.*

# Send us *your* interview story!

*Were you ever part of an interview — as candidate, interviewer, or recruiter — that was embarrassing, unforgettable, a comedy of errors, or somehow unusual?*

Send us the details: who, what, when, where and why. Describe the events, people, dialog and emotions.

What was the outcome and where are you now in your professional life?

Uplifting, happy-ending stories are especially encouraged.

Please include your phone number in case we have questions.

EDIN BOOKS *Inc.*

fax: 908-580-1008

email: 72417.627 @compuserve.com

mail: Edin Books, Inc. P.O. Box 59 Gillette, NJ 07933

**We'll send you a FREE book in which your story appears.**

# Index

Page numbers refer to the first page of the story in which the reference appears.

Page numbers refer to the first page of the story in which the reference appears.

Page numbers refer to the first page of the story in which the reference appears.

Page numbers refer to the first page of the story in which the reference appears.

Page numbers refer to the first page of the story in which the reference appears.

Page numbers refer to the first page of the story in which the reference appears.

Page numbers refer to the first page of the story in which the reference appears.

# About the Authors

**Gregory F. Farrell** is a corporate executive by profession, a storyteller and author by avocation. Currently chief financial officer for a multinational corporation headquartered in New Jersey, he has held financial management positions for 20 years in companies ranging from small to multibillion dollar multinationals. He also staffed an entire, newly organized division for a major health care manufacturing company. Greg's interviewing skills helped him come out of several corporate downsizings with better jobs at higher salaries. He has written extensively for *The Wall Street Journal's National Business Employment Weekly, Runner's World* and other business and lifestyle publications. His interest in people, their stories and job experiences began with his immediate family and expanded to international scope, leading to the development of this book. Greg holds a B.A. degree from Duke University and an M.B.A. from Columbia University. Originally from Stamford, Connecticut, he and his wife and two children live in New Jersey.

**Linda Sue Nathanson** is a writer, lecturer, psychologist and entrepreneur who is listed in six national and international *Who's Who* directories. Founder of The Edin Group, Inc., which provides résumé writing, technical writing and graphic design services, Linda has helped job seekers at every stage of their careers. Her résumé preparation articles have appeared in *The Wall Street Journal's National Business Employment Weekly* and other national and local publications. Trained as a research psychologist, she was twice a National Science Foundation Summer Research Fellow and held a post-doctoral research fellowship at the Albert Einstein College of Medicine. A series of résumé books featuring Rocky the Résumé™ is in progress. Linda earned M.A. and Ph.D. degrees from the University of California, Los Angeles and a B.S. from the University of Maryland. She lives in New Jersey with her husband and feline family.

**247**

**James F. Barrett**, president of ISES, Inc., a computer consulting firm, applies the wisdom gained over 25 years of staffing mission-critical strategic corporate projects to the "bottom lines" of this book. He has conducted thousands of interviews for in-house personnel and outside consultants. Author of the audio tape *Sock It To Them at the Interview* (see ad back of book), Jim has perfected a technique to select the best person for a job by matching personality and skills with job requirements. He holds an M.B.A. from Baruch University. A piano player and lover of classic rock-and-roll (late 1960s), "JB" and his wife live in New Jersey.

**Allan Varian** is a versatile writer/editor and a master of his craft. His 30-year career in communications touches all print and electronic publishing media. Direct experience writing/editing in a wide range of interest areas — from advertising, agriculture and education to chemicals, packaging and pharmaceuticals, finance, management and marketing — leavens his creative sense and has honed his editorial judgment and skills. Allan held communications management positions at several Fortune 500 companies until 1980 when he founded the communications consulting firm from which he recently took early retirement to pursue other personal and professional interests. He holds a B.A. degree from Rutgers University and lives with his wife in New Jersey.

**A.L. Sirois** is a writer, graphic artist/animator and musician who is listed in *Who's Who in the East*. His fantasy story *In the Conservatory* was nominated for the Pushcart Prize in 1990, and his children's book *Dinosaur Dress Up* was published in 1992 by Tambourine Press, a division of William Morrow & Co. He has also written advertising copy, book reviews and comic book scripts. Al, who is represented by the William Morris Agency, is a member of the Author's Guild, the Society of Children's Book Writers & Illustrators and the Science Fiction & Fantasy Writers of America. He is currently involved as a video game artist/animator, and performs as a percussionist with a jazz trio for which he also writes and arranges music. He and his wife Paula live with their two children in New York.

**Chris McDonough** blended his proven talent for illustration with a degree in psychology to draw Rocky the Résumé,™ the battered-bewildered, aggressive-triumphant cartoon character which has become the signature of Edin Books' "Rocky Series" of career development books, tapes and seminars. Chris is a sought-after freelancer who has also illustrated numerous children's books and countless advertisements. When not chained to his drawing board in the moonlight, he is senior art director of creative services for MarketSource Corporation. Chris is a graduate of Georgetown University, and lives with his wife and their son "where all roads meet" in central New Jersey.

**248**

# Everything you need to know about interviewing... to get the job you really want!

## Master the job interview process — once and for all.

*Among the topics covered in this powerful job-hunting seminar:*

- ✓ The one thing you should *never* say to an interviewer or recruiter

- ✓ The most common job interview mistakes — and how to avoid them

- ✓ A simple way to immediately create personal chemistry between you and the interviewer

- ✓ How to recover quickly and smoothly if you make a mistake

- ✓ Proven techniques for reducing stress and anxiety

- ✓ Best answers to the most commonly asked job-interview questions

- ✓ The three types of technical questions and how to answer them effectively

- ✓ Questions *you* can ask to make the interview more successful

- ✓ And much, much more....

### Jim Barrett
(your *career coach*)

James F. Barrett is an executive recruiter with more than 25 years' experience in interviewing and hiring candidates. Having conducted thousands of interviews, Barrett knows better than anyone what makes and breaks candidates in a job interview. Now he shares this knowledge to help you sock it to them at the interview—and get the job you really want.

***Gain an almost unfair advantage over other candidates.***

# Now, you can master the job interview process with this powerful 45-minute audio tape.

"Imagine having the job interviewer tell you, right before the interview, exactly what you have to do and say to pass the screening and get the job. That's what listening to *Sock It To Them At The Interview!* gives you — the right answers to difficult questions, from someone who has hired (and rejected) thousands of candidates. Invaluable!"

Robert W. Bly, author, *Creative Careers: Real Jobs in Glamour Fields*

"Jim Barrett staffed mission-critical strategic projects, conducting technical and personality interviews. He knew what questions to ask. We never had a candidate Jim selected wash out either for technical or personality reasons."

Russ DiFrancisca, former Director of MIS Emery-Purolator Worldwide

"I can always rely on Jim Barrett's interviewing skills and technical knowledge to select candidates who will become strong contributors."

Bob Berger, Vice President, major NYC bank

"With Jim Barrett's track record in picking candidates, I can't think of anyone I would rather take advice from if I wanted to build my own interviewing skills."

Yaron Inbar, Director, Sales Information and Automation, Bristol-Myers Squibb

## Go to job interviews with enthusiasm and confidence.

Put *Sock It to Them At The Interview!* in your cassette player. Listen to it on the way to your next interview. You'll immediately feel more prepared and confident — and you'll impress the interviewer with your crisp, sensible answers.

We're so sure that *Sock It to Them At The Interview!* will work for you, the tape comes with this unconditional money-back guarantee. If you're not satisfied for any reason, simply return the tape and we will refund your money — no questions asked.

*See Order Form on last page or call 800–334–6477.*

# ORDER FORM

**EDIN BOOKS** *Inc.*

P.O. BOX 59
GILLETTE, NJ
07933

PHONE
908·MIS–EDIN
908·647–3346

## Sold To:

☐ Let me know about pre-publication discounts on forthcoming books.

| NAME | ORDER DATE |
|------|-----------|

| COMPANY | |
|---------|--|

| ADDRESS | SUITE / APARTMENT # |
|---------|--------------------|

| CITY | STATE | ZIP |
|------|-------|-----|

## Ship To: if different from Sold To:

| NAME | |
|------|--|

| COMPANY | |
|---------|--|

| ADDRESS | SUITE / APARTMENT # |
|---------|--------------------|

| CITY | STATE | ZIP |
|------|-------|-----|

## Merchandise Ordered

| QUANTITY | PRODUCT DESCRIPTION | UNIT PRICE | TOTAL |
|----------|--------------------|-----------|-------|
| | *A Funny Thing Happened at the Interview* | $12.95 | $ |
| | *Sock It To Them at the Interview* (audio cassette) | $12.95 | $ |
| | Subtotal | | $ |
| | **6% Sales Tax** NJ RESIDENTS | | $ |
| | **Shipping** • $3 for first item | | $ 3.00 |
| | • Add'l items _____ x $1 ea. | | $ |
| | • Orders outside U.S. add $10 | | $ |
| | **TOTAL** | | $ |

## Method of Payment

☐ Check, payable to *Edin Books*

☐ Money order    ☐ MasterCard

☐ VISA    ☐ Amer. Express/Optima

| CARD NO | EXP. DATE |
|---------|-----------|

SIGNATURE

PHONE
(     )     ☐ Day ☐ Evening

*30-day unconditional money-back guarantee.*

FORM #AFTHI-95

## FAX Orders
24 hours a day
**908•580-1008**

## Phone Orders
9 am - 9 pm Eastern
**800•334-6477**